Garden Planning For The Small Property

Garden Planning For The Small Property

By JACK KRAMER

Drawings by CHARLES HOEPPNER
with Frank Chin Loy

CHARLES SCRIBNER'S SONS
New York

Drawing Credits:
Chapter 1. Sun Orientation Chart (Frank Chin Loy)
Chapter 2. Landscape Symbols (Frank Chin Loy)
Chapter 2. Garden Storage Shed (Frank Chin Loy)
Chapter 3. Constructing a Concrete Patio (Frank Chin Loy)
Chapter 3. Bricks on Sand (Frank Chin Loy)
Chapter 3. Garden Walks (Frank Chin Loy)
Chapter 4. Canvas Overhead (Frank Chin Loy)
Chapter 4. Wooden Overhead (Frank Chin Loy)
Chapter 4. Glass and Wood Fence (Frank Chin Loy)
Chapter 5. Texture and Leaf Pattern—Trees (Charles Hoeppner)
Chapter 5. Texture and Leaf Pattern—Shrubs (Charles Hoeppner)
Chapter 11. Modular Garden (Charles Hoeppner)

All run-around drawings by Charles Hoeppner

A - 2.72 [MZ]

Printed in the United States of America
Library of Congress Catalog Card Number 78-162771
SBN 684-12517-X (trade cloth)
SBN 684-12513-7 (trade paper, SL)

Acknowledgments

I wish to offer thanks to the many companies that have furnished helpful information and photos of their products for this book. These include:

California Redwood Association
California Association of Nurserymen
Westinghouse Electric Company
Scott Seed Company
Seymour Smith & Sons Tool Company
Lee L. Woodard Sons, Inc.

Personal gratitude is also given to Roger Scharmer, landscape architect, and Gary Patterson, landscape designer, who gave freely of their time and knowledge for this project. And once again a note of thanks to my capable artists, Charles Hoeppner and Frank Chin Loy, for their cooperation in this book.

Jack Kramer

Contents ✍

Introduction: THE SMALL GARDEN—
    YOUR PRIVATE RETREAT   1

1. YOUR PROPERTY AND YOU   3
        First Look at the Property
        Drainage and Grading
        Good Soil Makes the Difference

2. PLANNING THE SMALL GARDEN   11
        Planning on Paper
        Some Landscaping Fundamentals
        The Outdoor Room
        Approach to the House
        The Service Area

3. SURFACING THE SMALL GARDEN   23
        Patios and Terraces
        Paving Materials:
        Concrete, Brick, Precast Slabs,
        Flagstone, Indoor-Outdoor Carpeting,
        Walks and Steps

4. ENCLOSURES AND OVERHEADS   35
        Wood
        Overheads and Canopies

Walls and Fences
Stone Walls
Trellises

5. *PLANT MATERIALS AND HOW TO USE THEM*   49
Small Trees and Shrubs
Small Trees

6. *VINES FOR BEAUTY AND PRIVACY*   62
A Suitable Support
Vines as Garden Plants
List of Vines:
Twining Vines, Climbing Vines, Rapid-Growing
Vines, Vines for Flowers, Vines for Colorful Fruit

7. *THE FLOWER GARDEN (Annuals and Perennials)*   72
The Planting Plan (for Five- by Ten-Foot Area)
Color and Its Effect
Culture
Perennials and Biennials
Annuals

8. *CONTAINER PLANTS FOR SMALL GARDENS*   85
Containers
Tubs and Boxes
Caring for Container Plants:
Soil, Potting, Watering, Feeding
Plants to Grow
Shrubs for Container Gardening
Trees for Container Gardening

9. *THE SMALL CITY GARDEN*   97
Backyard Gardens
Doorway Gardens
The Tiny Terrace

Plant Materials That May Be Grown
   under City Conditions:
Deciduous Trees, Evergreen Trees, Deciduous
   Shrubs, Evergreen Shrubs, Vines

10. *SPECIAL GARDENS FOR SMALL AREAS*   107
   Herb Gardens
   Herbs for Fragrance
   Herb Chart
   Rose Gardens
   Planting and Care

11. *MODULAR GARDENS FOR PROBLEM AREAS*   117
   The Boxes
   Planting the Boxes
   Annuals
   Perennials
   Bulbs
   Shrubs and Trees for Modular
      and Deck Gardens

12. *BASIC MAINTENANCE*   128
   Composts
   Mulches
   Fertilization
   Pests and Diseases
   Pruning
   Tools and Equipment

APPENDIX
   Where to Buy Plants   139
   Helpful Reading   141
   Landscape Supplies   143
   State Agricultural Extension Services   145

Garden Planning
For The Small
Property

Introduction: The Small Garden— Your Private Retreat ✑

Today the average property is smaller than even a few years ago. Yet it is more important to our daily living than in former times. Even on a limited site most people want a garden, a retreat from a busy crowded world. Indeed, with land dwindling around us daily, your own special garden, small though it may be, is almost a necessity.

Landscaping as we knew it in the past—vast grounds of elaborate gardens—hardly exists now. Today's small property calls for clever arrangement and design to make it functional and eye appealing. It calls for low maintenance, yet beauty; low cost, yet functional space. New concepts of gardening are necessary to transform the small site into a functional beautiful setting to serve you and your family and at the same time be esthetically pleasing.

For the small garden it is essential to use appropriate trees and shrubs—plants that are in scale with the site. Pavings make the area seem larger and at the same time are inexpensive and easy to maintain. It is important to pick the best plants, for space does not allow too many errors.

This book is about planning the small garden to fulfill your needs whether it is a place for relaxing, for dining, or viewing as a pretty picture from the house. Designing the small property is framing your house with trees, shrubs, and flowers in a happy marriage of form, texture, and color.

If all this sounds like a big order from a small garden, read on. It can be done. In this book we hope to show and tell you how to do it reasonably and with low maintenance for maximum pleasure.

Jack Kramer

1

These attractive plantings—low ground cover and sculptural evergreens—set the pace for the overall landscape plan of beauty and eye appeal. The property is used wisely to create a handsome landscape picture from front to rear. Photo by Clint Bryant.

1. Your Property and You ℐ

Landscaping is basically shaping the property to your uses—additional space for dining, relaxing, or playing, or a place to grow plants. (At the same time it must create an esthetically inviting setting.) The basic premise of planning the property is putting it to work for you. What you want and how you shape it depends on the site, budget, weather, and climate.

If you can afford him, call in a landscape architect for a few consultations. This is not terribly expensive for a small property, and he can get you started. Then you can follow the plan with your own alterations for many years, since a good garden design is a result of time and thoroughness rather than haste and expediency.

A new property needs certain basics, such as drainage and grading, that will require attention before you do any planning. It is wise to start right—do the things that should be done and must be done—to avoid trouble later. You have probably heard this admonition a hundred times, but it is worth repeating.

For an old house, only minor attention to drainage and grading is generally necessary, for land curves and excess water drainage have already been well established.

First Look at the Property

Before you decide on any garden plan, walk your property several times. From the contractor's plot determine where the boundaries are, which way the site faces, and whether it is level or flat. Consider the view you have—if any—and seek out natural level changes that can be exploited to your benefit. Observe how close the neighbors are to see if you will need fences, screens, or hedges to ensure privacy. As you walk, make mental notes on whether the site is windy or calm and where there are protected areas and exposed places.

After "exploring" the property, go into the house and look at the site from a living-room window or any other rooms you occupy a good part of the time. Study the angles and vistas and seek out visually pleasing perspectives. Consider the lot as a space with small spaces within it, for a garden is several workable areas within one larger one.

If possible, visit neighbors' gardens and see what they have done. What kind of trees and shrubs have they used? Are their plantings thriving or just merely getting along? Nearby gardens, although in your same area, will not be identical. But they will be similar enough to give you an idea of what not to do. You will see things you like; remember these. Things you don't like, forget immediately.

Observe the shape of your property, for this is a clue to its arrangement. Is it long and narrow, rectangular, or pie-shaped; is it a corner site? The form is your starting point, because it dictates the shapes of patios and lawns and how they will relate to the overall form.

Drainage and Grading

As mentioned, an old house has little or no grading and drainage problems. The garden is established, and drainage patterns and run-off have been there a long time, saving you much money. Alterations, such as removing and replacing trees or shrubs and modifying the site somewhat, do require work and money, but it is little in comparison to the cost or time consumed in working out a garden plan for a new home.

A new house and grounds give you freedom in your garden design, but often grading is forgotten in the excitement of the purchase. Now is the time to observe and determine what has to be done.

Many new homes have a barren setting and compacted land from heavy equipment, so the grounds are not ready for landscaping. Generally, the contractor leaves you with graded subsoil—the topsoil has been stripped, and heavy machinery has compacted the soil. If the topsoil is still there (and it should be if you had a considerate contractor), it will be piled to one side some place.

If you want a small pool or a terrace, you will need level land; a

This small house utilizes the rear property area to advantage; it is private and a lush green picture. Yet there is little maintenance necessary and initial installation of plant material was inexpensive. Photo by Clint Bryant.

lawn requires a perfectly flat surface that has a slight pitch. Once the fence is up and shrubbery is in place, it is impossible to get equipment in to grade these areas. Determine now where you want the terrace, and decide where a flat surface for a lawn is needed.

The land around your house must be graded to slope away from the building and to carry water to the nearest street, storm drain, or watercourse. Be sure that the slope is in one direction, without rises or hollows. (Allow two inches to every ten feet.) Hollows will create bogs that will accumulate water and allow nothing to grow, and rises in the land are unsightly. Thus, rainwater *must* drain off your property.

Wait until after a good rainfall to determine just how to grade or how much to grade, for then you can see exactly which way the land lies and where the water goes. If you are fortunate, there may be no problems of standing water around the house or in the front or back yards. On the other hand, areas of subsoil several inches below the house must be filled, so that the slope of the land is not impeded.

To grade the property you will probably need the help of a bulldozer and front-end loader—an expensive job. If the area is reasonably small, you can tackle it with a shovel and rake and do it yourself in a few weeks.

Grading strips the topsoil from the land and leaves a subsoil base. The subsoil (after being bulldozed or raked to the desired depth) should be leveled, and the topsoil should be replaced. Before you put down topsoil, any soil compacted from heavy equipment will need turning and churning because plants will not grow in hard clay, which prevents water from getting to the roots.

Dwarf evergreens and low plantings were used here to create a quiet patio retreat completely in keeping with the character of the house. Further, because the site was small, the planting area too was kept in bounds and in proportion to the overall setting. Photo by Theodore Brickman; Hedrich-Blessing, landscape architects.

There are many kinds of topsoil. Get the best you can afford, as it pays off in lush green plants that need little care, rather than weak ones that always need attention. Inspect topsoil before buying and purchase from a reputable supplier to be sure of its quality. Topsoil should be black, crumbly, and porous (see below). Topsoil from unreliable sources is often soil excavated from another nearby site and is full of sticks, stones, and other debris. It is not mixed or screened. In my area they sell three different kinds of topsoil, ranging from $2.85 to $6.25 per cubic yard. Topsoil is delivered to the site by truck (eight or sixteen cubic yards) and is dumped at the site. (See Chapter 2, The Service Area, about deliveries.) You must do your own shoveling and spreading.

Good Soil Makes the Difference

Earth or soil has two layers—topsoil and subsoil. The subsoil beneath the surface layer has been there for hundreds of years. It can be from a few inches deep to twenty inches below the surface. Topsoil is composed of small particles of disintegrated rock, minerals, and decomposing organic matter and has living organisms, such as bacteria, fungi, and water, that hold the dissolved minerals, salts, and air. Most soils over the years lose their mineral content, and the soil must be reworked and revitalized.

Inspect the physical conditions of the subsoil around your house while it is exposed. Once it is covered with topsoil you will never know what lies beneath until plants refuse to grow and then die. If the subsoil is claylike, it will hold water too long and cause waterlogged sick plants. On the other hand, in sandy soils roots do not have a chance to absorb water. Now—not later—is the time to correct soil deficiencies.

It is difficult, but not impossible, to improve the conditions of clay soil. (Some plants do prefer moist or wet soils, but they are the exceptions.) Most clay soils will drain better if coarse concrete sand and humus is mixed into them.

Sandy soil is easy to work with and warms up quickly in the spring. However, it does not retain moisture, and many of the plant-soluble foods will be lost through leaching. Add liberal quantities of organic matter, humus, peat moss, and compost to improve a sandy soil.

Soil should be raked clean of debris and stones before planting. Condition your soil so that it is porous and crumbly to support good plant health. Photo courtesy of Scott Seed Company.

All soil must be reasonably loose and porous; it must breathe. Air must reach microorganisms and chemicals in the soil, and water must penetrate it.

It is time to add topsoil only after subsoils have been corrected. Most nurseries will tell you that a thin layer of topsoil is all that you need to grow plants. Don't believe it unless you are a stellar gardener! You will need at least four inches of topsoil; eight inches is better for lush trees and shrubs.

If the bulldozer is still available have the topsoil delivered immediately so that the operator can spread it for you. Otherwise, you must tediously transport the soil by wheelbarrow or bucket.

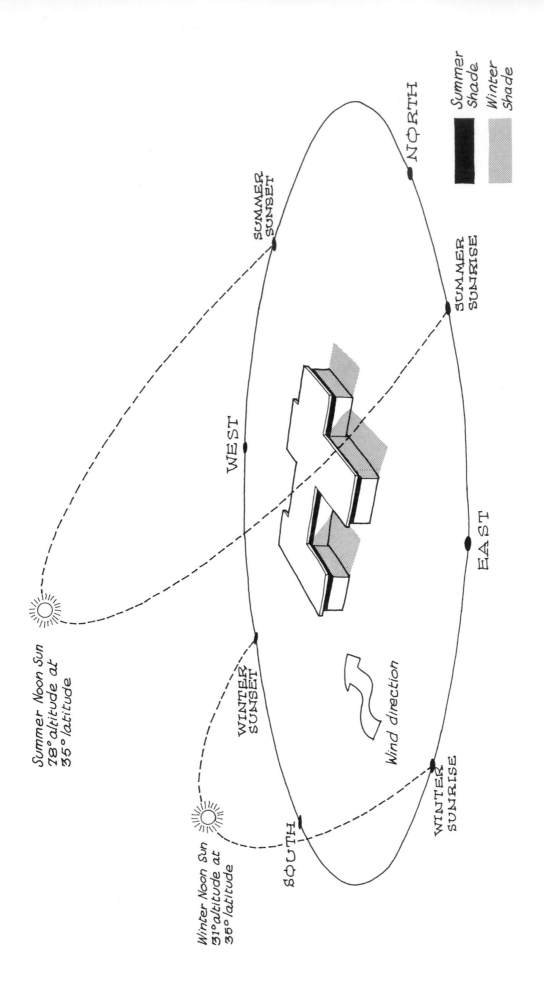

Summer Noon Sun
78°altitude at
35°latitude

Winter Noon Sun
31°altitude at
35°latitude

SUMMER
SUNSET

SUMMER
SUNRISE

NORTH

Summer
Shade

Winter
Shade

WEST

EAST

WINTER
SUNSET

Wind direction

SOUTH

WINTER
SUNRISE

SUN ORIENTATION CHART

2. Planning the Small Garden ✐

Every site is different; thus every garden plan is different. One of the joys of having your own home is that it is individual and how you design it is up to you. To begin to plan your property, it is wise to have a sketch on paper. First, make a plan of what you want the outdoor living space to do for you and what you can do for it to make it attractive.

Creating this plan is exciting. The arrangement you select and the plants you put into the ground—the entire picture is your very own. And in most parts of the country (without temperate all-year climate) it is a changing picture as seasons change. The plan you eventually select should be one which you can carry out over a period of years; it is not something to do in one season.

Laying out the garden involves the shapes and dimensions of the house and site, the functions and uses desired by the owners, and the plants and structural materials to be used.

PLANNING ON PAPER

A general ground plan of the property does not have to be drawn to scale; it can be a sketch. Try to obtain a plot plan showing the site dimensions. (Your builder can give you one.) Using this as your guide, transpose the location of the house and boundary lines onto graph paper. Let each square represent a foot. Draw an outline of the house, put in steps, walks, and driveways, and show existing trees and shrubs. Use basic landscape-design symbols for each item. (See drawing.)

Mark high and low areas on the paper. Show where there is sun-

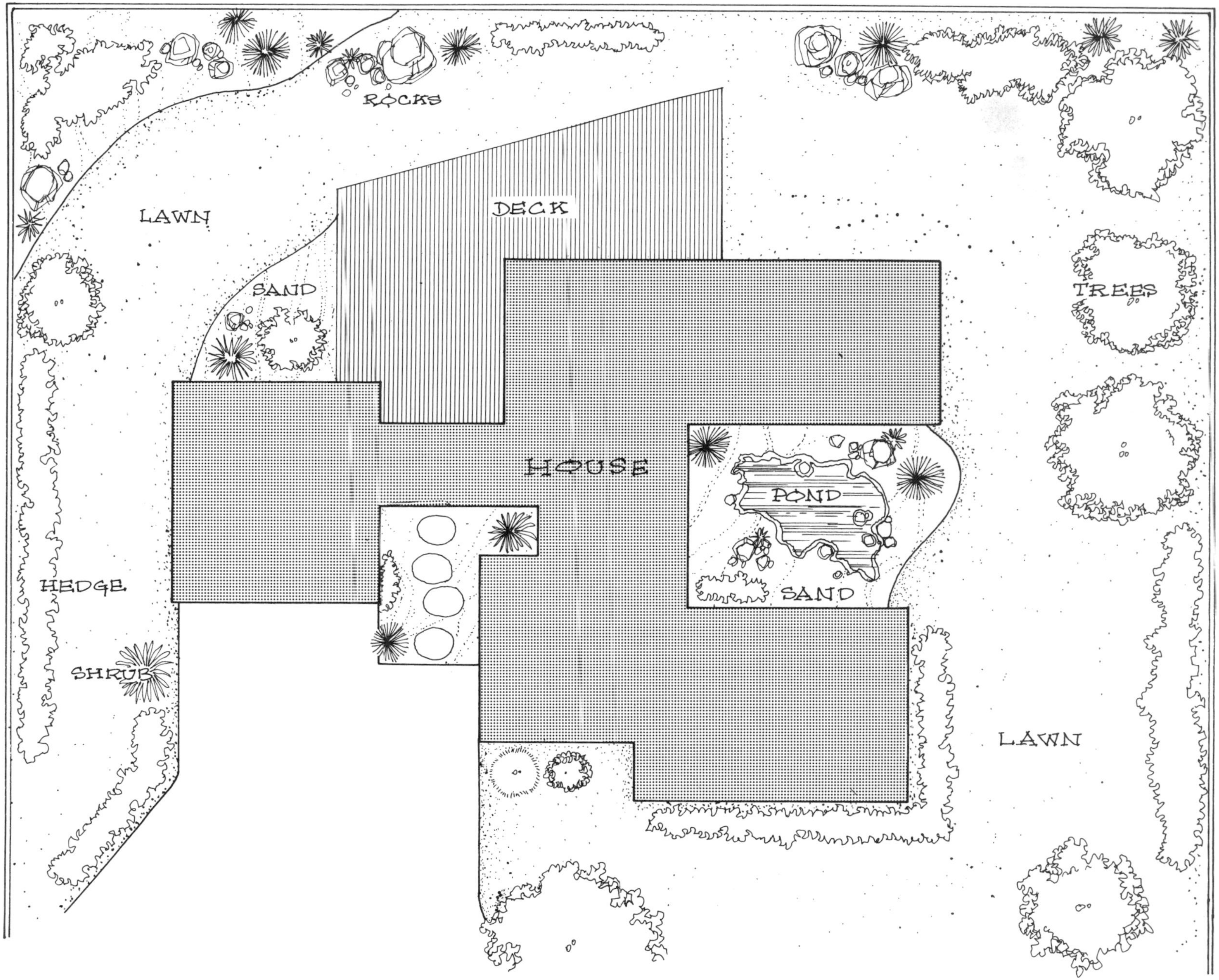

LANDSCAPE SYMBOLS

TREES

LAWN

POND

SAND

HOUSE

DECK

ROCKS

SAND

LAWN

HEDGE

SHRUB

light, shade, and the north point. Make a written list of the things you want on your property—dining area, terrace, view, fountain or pool, flower bed, hedges, and such absolutely essential things as walks and paths, driveways and garage, and play and work areas.

Over the graph paper lay a sheet of tracing paper, keeping the list of things you want at your side. Sketch traffic patterns first on the tracing paper. Then draw in the rough sizes and shapes of objects you want outdoors (terrace, garden beds, trees and shrubs, barbecue built-ins) and whatever else is necessary. Now the irregularly drawn shapes should start to relate to each other. If you are not pleased with the layout, start over on a new sheet of tracing paper. Consider all things carefully, and make several plans before going on to a detailed plan.

Once a satisfactory rough sketch is done, a detailed design is necessary. Exactness counts now, so be sure to have the proper measurements of the house and lot, objects, and existing plant material. Decide how much construction will be necessary in the garden —fences, screens, terraces, walls—and how much planting will be necessary.

SOME LANDSCAPING FUNDAMENTALS

To make full use of a small property, follow these fundamental rules:

1. Keep all elements in scale. Do not use large trees or shrubs for a small house or tiny plants for a large house.
2. Create one or two features for eye interest—for example, a terrace, a small fountain, or a lush area of drifts of flowers.
3. Do not overplant, but do put in enough plants to create an attractive setting in the second year. If you follow planting instructions for spacing plants from nurseries, it will take you four or five years to develop a handsome picture.
4. Suit the design to the character of the house and site.
5. Strive for a harmonious garden plan in which all objects are related. Do this by repeating shapes and employing the same materials.
6. Consider ground cover instead of a lawn, which usually requires constant maintenance..
7. If there is a slope on the site, take advantage of it for terracing.

8. Plan your property so that it does not require constant up-
keep.

The Outdoor Room

A patio or a terrace, even a small one, can serve as a place for dining outdoors, growing plants, or viewing, and should be near the
house for convenience. It can be on the side of the house, in the front,
or, as in most cases, in the rear of the property where there is generally space and privacy. Remember that this secluded area is your
quiet retreat.

The outdoor area does not have to be large, but it should be attractive and needs more care in planning than a large site. If possible,
break up the property into several patios. Keep each one a sensible
size, and treat them individually. One can be small and charming,
and another can be more elaborate. The shape of the outdoor area
also should be considered. Many patios are square or rectangular,
but there is no set rule; there are circular, elliptical, and free-form
shapes. The site, the architecture of the house, and personal tastes
dictate the patio design.

Almost any paving can be used as an outside floor. Tile and outdoor carpeting are popular now, but they are more costly than brick or concrete block. Because there are so many pavings available, select your materials and designs carefully. (See Chapter 3.)

Although a patio may be detached from a house, when integrated with the house it offers advantages. The living area is extended beyond the walls, and the inside rooms seem larger. Used as an occasional dining room, it is near the kitchen, and during parties it can accommodate an overflow of guests.

The patio or terrace is the outdoor area where you and your family will spend the most time, so make it pleasant and private. It can become the most important living space of the home many months of the year.

APPROACH TO THE HOUSE

The approach to the house, usually referred to as the front yard, has been neglected, and yet it is here that a visitor receives his first impression of what is to come. Necessity often dictates an open front yard, but the small enclosed court or entry patio should not be ignored. The front of the house may be a better garden site than the rear when:

1. A steep hill slopes down to the rear of the house.
2. The house is far back from the lot line.
3. Neighbors' windows overlook the rear.
4. The front view is good.
5. The sun-wind relationship is better in the front.

Enclosing the front of your property may seem unconventional; however, it is an old idea borrowed from English manor and Spanish country houses. The enclosed yard provides a pleasant and effective entrance through a private garden, and the overall setting for the house is greatly enhanced. Fences today are no longer massive and unsightly or expensive. There are many materials besides wood with which to make fences. Concrete blocks are available in many patterns and are easy to install; bricks are always charming, but a brick fence requires professional skill to build.

Once you decide on an entry court garden, consider the same principles of design and arrangement as for the rear area: a private

The approach to this house is in keeping with the cottage effect of the landscape plan; it is small and charming yet not ostentatious, colorful yet not dramatic. Photo by Jack Roche.

Handsome plantings and screenings, a well-designed overhead, and attractive stone combine to make a service-driveway area exceedingly pleasing and yet very functional. Photo by Clint Bryant.

The approach to this small garden is simple, yet attractive; the lot size is 50 by 100 feet. Photo by Roger Scharmer.

The approach to this small house is a charming rock stairway; it's a natural scene that is interesting and pleasing to incoming guests. Photo by Roger Scharmer.

place, the appearance of the area in relation to the house, and the selection of proper plant materials placed strategically. In the front, landscaping becomes a setting for the house and a garden; it is a dual area. A large house demands specimen plants; for a smaller house, container plants are suitable as long as they are in scale with the architecture and in harmony with all other plantings.

THE SERVICE AREA

This area is often neglected, but it is the heart of the plan. Trash cans, clotheslines, tool sheds, and the vegetable and cutting gardens are all part of the service region. Here too is the garage or carport and the driveway. Trucks will deliver building materials "tailgate," which means to your driveway only; moving and hauling takes time and hard work and is expensive if you have to hire someone to do it.

Try to screen trash or garbage cans from view; use sunken cans or a small box with a wooden top. If possible, keep the cans in the garage or perhaps at a small angle in the fence so that they are hidden. Even though garbage cans should be close to the kitchen so that there is a minimum of carrying, be sure to put them far enough from the house so that odors do not permeate the house or terrace.

Today driveways and garages are a planning lesson in themselves; they must have design and spacing to be functional. Make driveways wide enough for vehicles, and definitely have a car turnaround; it is essential for owners and guests. Try not to have the driveway to the garage on a steep grade; excavate or fill it if possible to obtain greater safety. Never slope the driveway toward the house. If you do, rainwater will flow directly into the garage. It is a good idea to frame the driveway with shrubs, but be sure that you select low-growing ones so that they won't obscure the view of oncoming cars.

Make a carport at least fifteen by twenty-five feet with a hard-surfaced floor—concrete or asphalt. Allow a gentle slope for the roof so that water can run off easily. Use gutters or downspouts from the roof into a drain line, to prevent soil erosion around the carport. Most carports are bare and look unsightly, so add some pot plants for charm. It takes but a few minutes to make this structure a handsome addition to the plan rather than an eyesore.

Since garden power and hand tools are necessary, and often storing and hauling them to the site is hard work, a utility shed should

Simple but useful is this deck and sand area used as a play space for children. The deck area is portable, and the sand pit can be filled in with concrete when the play area is no longer wanted and children are grown. Photo courtesy of California Redwood Association.

be near the garden area. These sheds should have closable doors. Commercial sheds can be purchased, or you can make your own.

If it is not possible to have a closed storage shed, try screening this utilitarian area. Hedges and fences are enough protection if tools must be left outdoors. Of course, in the winter they will have to be stored in a closed area, such as the garage.

20

GARDEN STORAGE SHED

This shed is a combination storage of garden equipment, potted plants and also has a barbecue cabinet, with garbage disposals. It's a place to store all your gardens tools, and also such large equipment as a power mower and wheel barrow. Work counters are provided with shelves above and beneath it.

Perforated hardboard, nailed to studs, accommodates smaller tools. The barbecue cabinet keeps all the necessary equipment, including a space and place for a hibachi. Potted plants are stored on shelves in a small greenhouse.

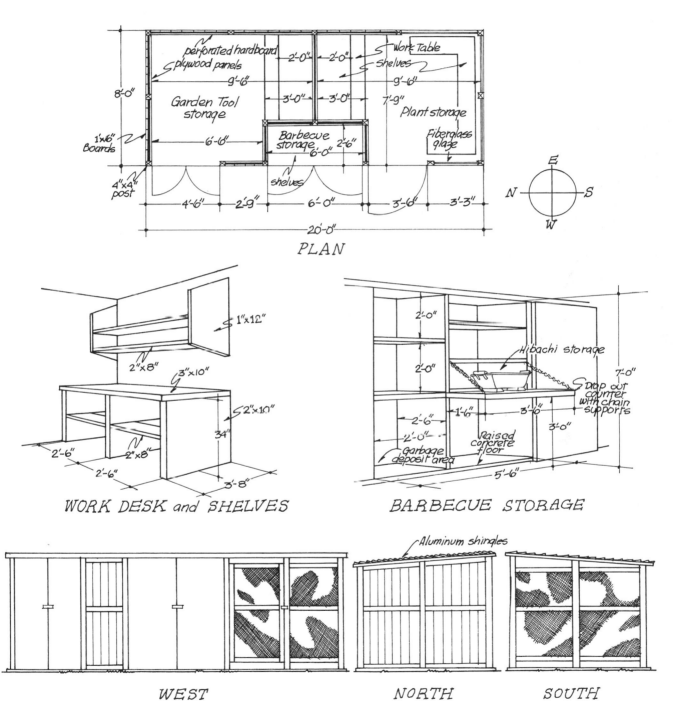

PLAN

WORK DESK and SHELVES

BARBECUE STORAGE

WEST

NORTH

SOUTH

ELEVATION

Flagstone accents this patio-porch; the lovely texture sets off the lush lawn.
Photo by Molly Adams.

3. Surfacing the Small Garden ✐

Surfacing is an important part of planning a small property. Too often people put down a slab of concrete for a patio or terrace and then are disappointed when the outdoor living area is sterile and uninviting. The paved area must be a part of the total design and fit into the picture. And remember that paved areas need only an occasional washing rather than planting and maintenances.

PATIOS AND TERRACES

Today a patio or terrace is almost essential for the outdoor area. It can be an excavated place filled with gravel or stone, but more likely it will be an area that is paved for esthetic reasons. The paving material can be brick or concrete, tile or flagstone, carpeting or precast slabs, or patio blocks. Each has character, texture, usefulness, and appeal; how you put it all together is what makes a garden attractive. Depending on the surfacing used, patterns can vary immeasurably. Remember that pavings are usually geometrically shaped—squares, rectangles, octagons—and pleasing patterns will create an eye interest that lessens monotony and provides decorative accent. Blocks or bricks can be laid in infinite patterns, but keep the patterns simple and attractive; the overdesigned terrace floor can be as upsetting as the overpatterned living-room carpet. It will detract from, rather than enhance, the garden setting, so sketch several patterns before you start. Surfacing can add more charm and character for less money than plantings and other features.

Try to blend whatever type of material you select with the existing materials—in the house or the boundaries—and with borders

23

and plant containers. In other words, repeat the patterns or materials throughout the garden; this gives an illusion of space.

For economy and easy installation the square or rectangular patio is best. Paved curved areas are more costly and take more time to install because paving slabs and blocks must be cut.

The actual paving area depends on the house and lot size and how it is going to be used. For patios make the area reasonably large so that it is usable (at least fourteen by twenty feet for an average home). The patio should, if possible, adjoin the living or dining room.

When you are considering the available paving materials, check them against the following questions:

1. Will the surface level off smoothly for quick drainage?
2. Will the paving produce glare?
3. Will the paving be slippery when wet? (Concrete is.)
4. Does the material harmonize with the house and garden structures?
5. Can the floor be easily maintained?
6. Can the surfacing be laid at a reasonable cost?
7. Will the floor be weather resistant?
8. Can you do some of the work yourself? (Some floors are easy to install; others need heavy equipment.)

PAVING MATERIALS

Concrete

Concrete makes a satisfactory patio floor, with some modifications. As mentioned, it needs design and thought. Developers have a habit of throwing down a slab of concrete against one house wall and calling it a patio. This large surface is rarely attractive, soon cracks, and is slippery.

If you use concrete, divide the space into squares—six- to eight-feet squares. Larger squares require reinforcing to prevent cracking. Filling between the squares is not necessary if you allow each one to set before laying the next one; however, for looks you might want to use wood strips between the concrete.

If the gray color of concrete is monotonous, use a coarse gravel

CONSTRUCTING A CONCRETE PATIO

The concrete formula recommended for garden paving is 1 part cement, 2¼ parts sand, and 3 parts gravel or crushed rock. Add about 5 gallons of water for each sack of cement used. The water should be clean

and pure, the sand must be clean river sand, and the gravel or crushed rock should be 1" maximum in size.

Mark out area to be paved, then remove sod and soil. Use tamper to compact the soil and make it fairly even and smooth.

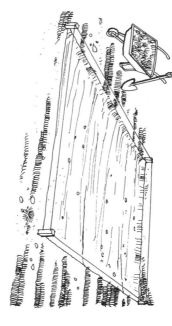

Secure edgings by driving stakes slightly lower than height of edgings and nail securely with galvanized nails. Spread sand evenly to a depth of 2 inches, then dampen it by fine spray to help it settle.

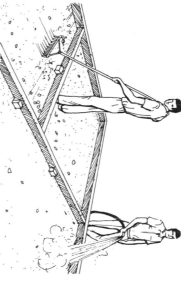

Cover dividers that are to be left in place with a layer of masking tape before pouring the concrete. Leave stakes in place.

Pour concrete into one section at a time. Rake the concrete well into the corners; overfill the forms slightly. Use straightedge to strike-off concrete so its level is with height of forms.

Trowel concrete with a steel float for a denser smooth surface. Use bristle broom for texture, and provides good traction.

Cover with plastic to seal in moisture of curing, for at least five days.

aggregate in the concrete to eliminate the sterile look and add texture to the area.

Brick

Brick has a natural look, is attractive outdoors, and provides a nonglare, nonskid surface. It is easy to install and inexpensive, and comes in different patterns and colors. It can be used in combination with other hard flooring materials for a handsome effect. It is an ideal paving with but one drawback: when covered with water, frequently it becomes coated with algae and can be slippery.

Brick comes in a variety of earthy colors, rough or smooth surfaced, and glazed or unglazed. Different shapes are available (hexagonal and octagonal, for example), but they must be used with caution because shaped bricks require precise installation and manipulation of pattern.

The best patio bricks are smooth-surfaced or rough-textured common brick. Select hard-burned instead of green brick; it is dark red rather than the salmon color that indicates an underburned process and less durability. Used bricks are fine too if you can locate them, but often, because of their natural look, they are more expensive than new brick. Be sure the dealer has enough of the brick you select to complete the floor, for usually there are some dimensional variations and color differences in later brick purchases.

To save money, you can install a brick-on-sand paving. It is not difficult, but does require patience. Mark out the site with string and stakes; then excavate, grade, and level the ground. Put in a perfectly level sand base of three inches. (The floor will be wavy and visually distracting if the ground is not level.) Do the floor in sections, a small piece at a time, rather than trying to do the whole area in a day.

To cut bricks, use a cold chisel or a brick hammer. Cut a groove along one side of the brick and give it a sharp, severing blow. Smooth uneven edges of the brick by rubbing them with another brick.

On the three-inch sand base set the bricks in place as closely

Small but lovely is this intimate garden; hanging plants on the house walls and foliage specimens along the fence make the area seem larger than it is. Note that large plants are not used, as they would be out of scale with the small house. Photo by Roger Scharmer.

The author's patio has an almost tropical setting that provides a colorful display. There is ample space for sitting and relaxing or sunning. The paving is concrete aggregate. Photo by Joyce R. Wilson.

together as possible, and check each row with a level. Dust sand into the cracks. Slope the floor away from the house at an incline of one inch per six feet of paving.

Bricks can be laid in herring-bone, basketweave, running-bond, soldier-course, and stretcher-bond patterns, or combine them with grass squares or cinders in endless designs. In large areas use the herring-bone pattern; smaller patios look best with a running-bond or basketweave pattern. For very large areas use redwood or cedar grids between the bricks for a handsome effect.

Brick can be set in mortar, but this is usually a job for a professional bricklayer.

Precast Slabs

Precast slabs are very popular and come in a variety of colors and sizes. They are inexpensive and easy to install, and provide a nonslip durable surface. The slabs are available in one-and-one-half-inch and two-inch thicknesses.

Be wary of the very colorful slabs; when they are mixed with other landscape colors, the result often is too garish. Test the color of the slab when both wet and dry, for there is quite a difference.

Slabs can be installed in many patterns. Mix sizes for a random block effect, use one size, or try some of the hexagonal or circular shapes. Remember that the jointing has to be done with precision care.

Excavate enough to allow for a three-inch sand base and the thickness of the concrete block. The blocks can be laid on the sand base or on concrete and joined together with mortar for more durability. You can butt-joint the blocks by putting them in place as closely together as possible and filling the interstices with mortar. Or you can use a dry mix filling (brush a dry sand and cement mixture at the rate of five to one between the joints when the slabs are laid). Spray with water afterwards and allow to set.

Precast slabs of concrete aggregate panels are also available; install in the same manner.

Flagstone

Flagstone is either square or rectangular and gives a rich lifetime surface. The irregularity of the material is part of its charm, and its

HOW TO SET BRICKS ON SAND

This method is the easiest for the beginner. Most of these operations as shown below also apply to laying bricks over existing concrete, and in wet or dry mortar.

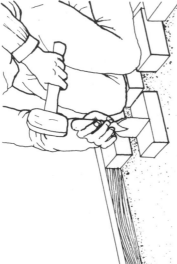

Lay the bricks on the sand carefully so it would not disturb it and become uneven. Work forward from bricks already laid. After paving a small section move the edging over. Tap any high bricks into the sand with a rubber mallet or a hammer handle. Cut bricks for fit by holding wide chisel in place, and using heavy mallet, for a firm tap.

Six different patterns for brick laying.

Running Bond

Jack-on-Jack

Basket Weave

Half Basket

Double Basket

Diagonal Herringbone

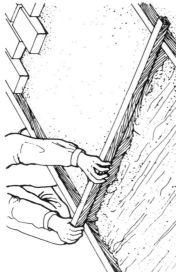

With edgings in place turn over soil and pulverize it. Using a screed (a 2"x4" that rides on the edgings with an extension which levels the sand) level the sand about three feet at a time. For adequate drainage, grade area to slope at least one inch every six feet, then roll it until it is hard and flat.

Using a hose nozzle that gives a fine spray, wet the area to settle the sand between the cracks.

Using 1"x4"s or 2"x4"s start constructing a wooden framework around the entire area to be paved. Then divide the framed area with a temporary edging into smaller sections, these sections can run the length of the area. Spread sand between edgings to a depth of 1" to 2". Then wet the sand with a fine spray to settle it.

Throw handfuls of fine sand out across the bricks and let it dry completely in the sun for a few hours. Then sweep it into the cracks.

Used brick is the paving material for this small attractive garden area. Photo by Roger Scharmer.

colors—buff, brownish red, and gray—add warmth to the patio. Flagstone is hard stratified stone (shale, slate, or marble) split into flat pieces that can be installed dry or in mortar. For masonry use one-inch thick stone; for dry laying, use one-and-one-half-inch stone.

If the ground is well drained and level, flagstones can be installed directly on it. (They will shift somewhat in very cold weather, but will remain in place.) For a sturdier and better floor, set the flagstones in sand; a two-inch bed is fine. Firmly place the flags over the entire surface and make sure that they are really in place, so that no listing will occur. Fill in the joints with soil that is flush with the surface of the stones, and wet it down thoroughly.

For a permanent paving, set flags on a three-inch concrete bed.

INDOOR-OUTDOOR CARPETING

Indoor-outdoor carpeting is very popular and is now made in easy-to-install blocks of various sizes and colors. However, it can and does stain, and after a while it deteriorates and has to be re-

31

placed. Furthermore, although it is beautiful in the home, it generally looks odd when used outdoors. It is good, though, around pools because it provides a nonskid, soft surface. It can also be used effectively for small patio areas, but for large expanses hard surfacing looks better, lasts longer, and needs little maintenance.

Walks and Steps

Walks and paths are necessary so that you can move around your garden with ease. Brick, precast stone slabs, wood rounds, cinder, gravel, and fir bark are all good materials for paths, but it is important to use them in harmony with the garden plan. For instance, in a woodsy setting, wood rounds or fir bark add warmth and charm; concrete would be out of place. While it is essential to have paths, either make them as unobtrusive as possible or, make them an integral part of the plan. To do this, repeat the pattern and material elsewhere in the garden so the plan is coordinated.

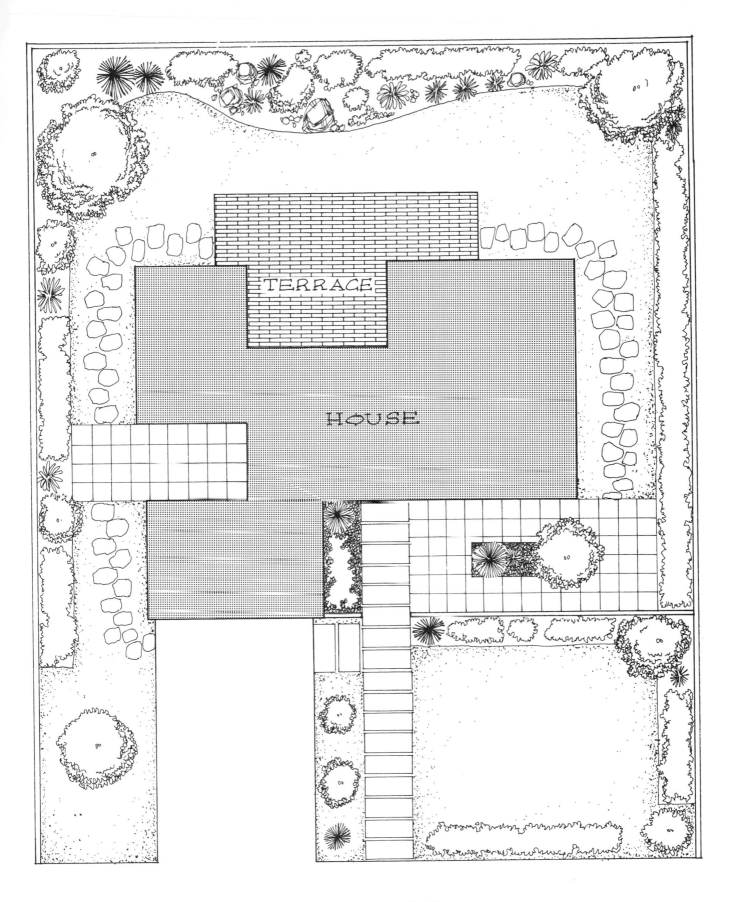

GARDEN WALKS

A path to the house is another garden necessity; it must be direct, well paved, and wide enough for two people to walk side by side. A six-foot width is generally suitable. A wide shallow step in front of the door adds charm to the scene and is a place for container plants in summer.

While a curved path is certainly feasible and adds grace to the plan, a straight walk is acceptable too. Any patio surfacing—brick, tile, concrete blocks—can also be used for walks. Install brick or concrete blocks on a level bed of sand or cinders to allow water to seep through. Use a three-inch bed of cinders and then add a one-inch layer of sand. Unless bricks are installed as closely together as they can be, they will become loose. With whatever paving you use, drain underneath deep and well.

Steps are dramatic accents in a garden and should be used more. They can break the monotony of a large site, and there are infinite arrangements. They may be irregular with various angles and turns and interestingly shaped islands. A wide tread and a short rise are best for garden steps; a fifteen-inch tread with a rise of about five to six inches is a good average.

Try to avoid too many steps in one area; it is best to use two or three of them where a change of levels is necessary and repeat the arrangement later.

34

4. Enclosures and Overheads ✍

A garden plan involves more than plants and flowers; in its overall design, man-made structures play an important part too. Fences and screens of various materials are desirable because they create a feeling of seclusion and they act as a shield against wind and (sometimes) neighbors. Overheads and canopies are often necessary in the small garden for sunlight, glare, and rain protection, and the patio or terrace that has a partial or complete ceiling can be used more than an open patio.

Trellises and lattices are other garden accents. They can be used as walls (covered with vines) or as decoration, the wood patterns pleasing to the eye and adding dimension to the scene.

Unless you hire someone to do it, generally you will have to build your own enclosures, overhangs, and trellises. However, even the novice with only a smattering of basic construction details and knowledge of wood can do it.

Wood

Wood is the basic building material for most garden accessories. It is readily available, moderately priced, and easy to work with. Lumber is sold in a variety of grades and stock sizes (see Tables 1 and 2), and it is wise to know something about the material, so that you can get the most for your money and the best kinds and sizes for your job.

The best quality or grade of lumber is free of knots and blemishes and is smoothly finished. It is rarely necessary to use this grade for fences or overhangs because knots and other defects will not affect

Standard Dimensions of Surfaced Lumber

THICKNESS		WIDTH		SQUARES	
Rough	Surfaced	Rough	Surfaced	Rough	Surfaced
1″	25/32″	3″	2–⅝″	3 x 3″	2–⅝ x 2–⅝″
1–¼″	1–1/16″	4″	3–⅝″	4 x 4″	3–⅝ x 3–⅝″
1–½″	1–5/16″	5″	4–⅝″		
2″	1–¾″	6″	5–⅝″	5 x 5″	4–⅝ x 4–⅝″
3″	2–⅝″	8″	7–½″	6 x 6″	5–⅝ x 5–⅝″
		10″	9–½″		
4″	3–⅝″	12″	11–½″	8 x 8″	7–½ x 7–½″

Table for Converting Linear to Board Feet

LUMBER SIZE	LINEAR FEET								
	8	10	12	14	16	18	20	22	24
1 × 2	Sold by linear foot								
1 × 3	Sold by linear foot								
1 × 4	2–⅔	3–⅓	4	4–⅔	5–⅓	6	6–⅔	7–⅓	8
1 × 6	4	5	6	7	8	9	10	11	12
1 × 8	5–⅓	6–⅔	8	9–⅓	10–⅔	12	13–⅓	14–⅔	16
1 × 10	6–⅔	8–⅓	10	11–⅔	13–⅓	15	16–⅔	18–⅓	20
1 × 12	8	10	12	14	16	18	20	22	24
2 × 2	Sold by linear foot								
2 × 3	Sold by linear foot								
2 × 4	5–⅓	6–⅔	8	9–⅓	10–⅔	12	13–⅓	14–⅔	16
2 × 6	8	10	12	14	16	18	20	22	24
2 × 8	10–⅔	13–⅓	16	18–⅔	21–⅓	24	26–⅔	29–⅓	32
2 × 10	13–⅓	16–⅔	20	23–⅓	26–⅔	30	33–⅓	36–⅔	40
2 × 12	16	20	24	28	32	36	40	44	48
3 × 6	12	15	18	21	24	27	30	33	36
4 × 4	10–⅔	13–⅓	16	18–⅔	21–⅓	24	26–⅔	29–⅓	32

the strength or appearance of the fence. For most garden structures use rough-finished lumber; it is moderately priced and suitable for almost all projects.

Redwood, cedar, and cypress (in that order) are the best woods for outdoor use. Redwood weathers beautifully and needs no preservative coating. Cedar and cypress will last many years without preservatives, but generally they should be given protective coatings. (Preservative solutions are sold at lumber and hardware stores.)

There are many fence and screen designs, but basically you will need only posts, rails, and boards. Posts should be about two feet longer than the height of the fence. Solid board fences need longer posts because more weight is involved; figure the length at three and one-half feet longer than the fence height.

For most enclosures, four- by four-inch posts are fine and for gates and corner posts use eight- by eight-inch posts. Rails or stringers as they are some times called, may be two by four's; they should have post supports every eight feet. Two by four rails are suitable for most fences unless they are very heavy. In that case choose three- by four-inch rails.

Popular fence board sizes are one by six or one by eight inches. For solid surface fences one- by eight-inch or one- by ten-inch boards are best.

OVERHEADS AND CANOPIES

Overheads and canopies vary greatly in design and material, but basically they are for protection against sun or for privacy if there are neighbors overhead. They may be a partial covering of canvas strips or an eggcrate or lath-design ceiling that allows some sun, some shade. With ceilings, determine just how much sun you will need for plants and how much shade for comfort.

A popular overhead is lattice and lath, which affords protection from wind without stopping vertical air circulation. A simple lath roof is easy to build with two- by two-inch lumber, spaced about two inches apart and supported by two- by ten-inch beams. Support the roof with two- by six-inch posts, spaced two feet apart and set on concrete piers.

Louvered boards make another suitable garden overhang; space them one inch apart. Or you might want to try one-fourth-inch

Top: *This photo shows the beauty of a lath-type overhead; it affords perfect lighting conditions for plants and for people.* Photo by Joyce R. Wilson.

A unique canvas overhead protects this terrace from sun. The shelter is highly contemporary and well suited to the semicircular benches and concrete aggregate paving. Photo courtesy of National Cotton Council.

CANVAS OVERHEAD

Canvas is used again in this deck picture. Here it is an eave design, exceptionally pretty and well suited to the area. Photo by Phil Palmer, courtesy of California Redwood Association; Royston, Hanamoto & Mayes, landscape architects.

This patio doubles as a plant room; there is adequate area for plants and people. The floor is brick, the overhang glass and redwood. Photo by Joyce R. Wilson.

plywood. It is available bent or woven and can be sawed to almost any shape.

Woven canvas strips in a basket-weave design construct an overhead easily assembled once the wood frame is up. Use posts in preset concrete piers and be sure the frame is rigid; then lace canvas over and under the beam supports.

WALLS AND FENCES

Wood harmonizes well with outdoor settings; it is the most popular fencing material and can be constructed in many designs. You can paint or stain wood, leave it raw to mellow with weather, or combine it with such materials as woven plywood, plastic panels, and tempered glass. Canvas strips may also be used for an interesting effect.

You need a garden line, yardstick, and post-hole digger (rented from a hardware store) to build a fence. Depending on the type of fence, posts should be set four to eight feet apart. Dig holes deep (eighteen to twenty-four inches) and treat wood with a preservative. Be sure that the posts are set straight in the holes; use a level.

Fences can be of several designs: a two-way louver type—two- by four feet boards set on two- by four-feet stringers with three-fourth-inch dadoes at 45° angles; a solid board with the boards nailed edge to edge; a shadow box with the boards nailed to stringers on the front and back, spaced just less than a board apart; a two way with vertical boards alternated first on one side and then nailed on the other side; a skip space with the boards secured horizontally and spaced one board apart; a basketweave with one-inch boards nailed to one post, passed on opposite side of another post, and nailed again to the third post; a novelty accordion type with the boards placed in a "vee" pattern for every six-foot panel; and, of course, innumerable patterns you yourself design.

Plastic panels of corrugated design can be nailed to posts and stringers, or use glass inserts in wooden frames.

Masonry materials—concrete blocks or bricks—can be used for walls; they are durable and have decorative appeal.

When they are part of the garden design, walls do much to enhance the overall landscape beauty. They blend well with both contemporary and formal homes. Walls do not need to be complete enclosures; I have seen many handsome brick-wing walls used as

This photo of a lath-type overhead demonstrates excellent lighting conditions. Photo by Joyce R. Wilson.

A simple wooden fence frames a lawn and concrete patio. Installation is easy and material inexpensive. Photo by Joyce R. Wilson.

Redwood solved multiple problems in this garden site; it is used for decking, fence, and overhead. The fence is simple but attractive, the laths spaced one-half-inch apart to create a dimensional effect, and the overhead structure repeats the rectangular design of the floor. Photo courtesy of California Redwood Association; Ned Rucker, landscape architect.

Here a hedge is used in place of a fence; note the privacy provided by the plantings. It is indeed a sylvan retreat. Photo by Roger Scharmer.

WOODEN OVERHEAD

For a more formal property a brick wall painted white creates charm and appeal. At the same time it provides a necessary horizontal line in the garden and is in perfect character with the overall plan. Photo by Molly Adams; L. A. Ireys, landscape architect.

eye interest to create a charming feature with potted plants placed on them.

Buy ready-mix mortar for wall construction. Put it on a smooth surface, and mix it thoroughly with water until the mortar slips easily off the trowel. If the mortar dries while you are working with it, add more water. For best results, mix small amounts many times rather than one large quantity.

When constructing a wall of concrete blocks, you must use a poured concrete footing. Make the footing deep, so that there won't be a possibility of a break in the wall. Check local building codes to determine the frost line in your area. Place blocks about half an inch apart, and number them for easy installation. Wet down the foundation, apply mortar, and set your first block. Place the block dry, and tap it gently with your trowel handle to set it in place; then smear the ends of the block with mortar. Set the blocks to the end of the row, lining them up and leveling them as you proceed.

Keep all cement work moist for a few days to allow a slow cure to prevent cracks. And don't use mortar when temperatures are below

40°F. because it will only cause cracking in the wall. You can paint the wall if you desire; there are many new colors for masonry.

Do investigate the new concrete blocks that are available in a variety of decorative themes—fleur-de-lis, Mediterranean, and Moorish. They can be left natural or painted. They make handsome accents, and putting them up is an easy job—no more difficult than using concrete block.

Brick walls also need a foundation. Again, check the frost line and install the appropriate foundation. Never lay dry bricks. Put mortar on the footing for the first course or row. Using your trowel upside down, press ripples into the mortar; this gives a good gripping surface for the brick. Remove excess mortar with the edge of the trowel. Lay the first brick for the second row, and use the trimmed mortar to smear the edge of the next brick. Be sure to keep the rows of bricks even and level. Remove all loose bits of mortar from the wall before they have a chance to set. Cover the brick wall with wet burlap for a few days to permit a slow cure and to prevent cracks. When you clean the walls with muriatic acid a few weeks later, hose them thoroughly.

STONE WALLS

The many types of stones for walls—rubble, fieldstone, and cut stone—are not easy to work with. Most are irregularly shaped, so

Here a concrete block fence is part of the garden. The design is interesting and handsome. It allows light and cooling breezes into the patio and yet you cannot see through it. Photo by Kenneth Kavana, courtesy of National Concrete Masonry Association.

GLASS AND WOOD FENCE

One way to provide privacy and control wind without completely cutting off the view is to use glass in movable louvered frames and lath screens. Each glass frame pivots on an ordinary nail and friction holds it in place. Drill a hole through the top and bottom rails for each frame slightly larger than the nail. Put the screen in place and hammer a nail through the holes into each screen frame. In making the lath screens, you can get a uniform parallel spacing between lath strips using a spacer. Use two nails on each end of each lath.

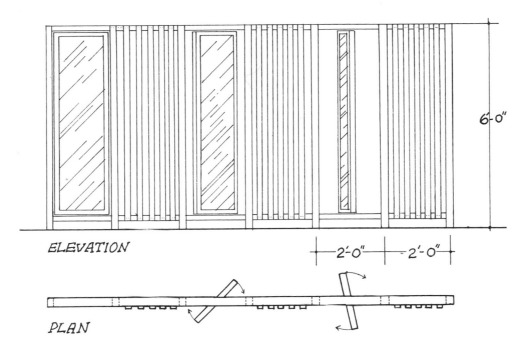

ELEVATION

6'-0"

2'-0"   2'-0"

PLAN

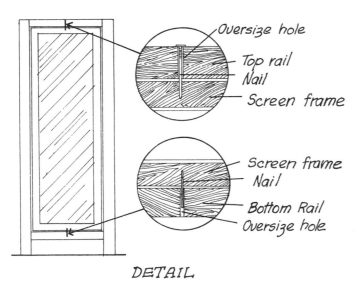

Oversize hole
Top rail
Nail
Screen frame

Screen frame
Nail
Bottom Rail
Oversize hole

DETAIL

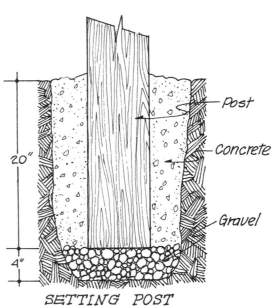

Post
Concrete
Gravel

20"

4"

SETTING POST

you must cut and break the stones to make them fit properly. I suggest that this type of wall be done by the professional.

TRELLISES

Recently, both indoor and outdoor trellising has become immensely popular; the design and Victorian feeling has caught the public's fancy. Trellises have charm, but they are not easy to put together. Although commercial ones are available, the handcrafted ones look more attractive.

A trellis is an openwork wood structure. It can be used on walls, in front of windows, or in an unsightly corner to hide a cracked wall, or as roofing for patios, as a decorative accent, or as a support for vines. The one-inch-wide slats are generally redwood strips or laths. The overall size of the trellis must be considered before the design can be determined. For large areas, more negative space is desirable; for small areas the lathing can be close together.

Overhead trellising lets light and air through, but still provides shade. A trellis against a wall is strictly decorative; with lovely vines it becomes functional.

An unpainted redwood trellis is attractive, but a coat of white paint makes it dazzling. If you do paint a trellis, however, have patience, for it is a tedious job whether done before or after it is assembled. Don't use spray-on paint; it costs a fortune to cover an average trellis. It is best to paint with a narrow brush.

5. Plant Materials
and How to Use Them

We are all familiar with shrubs and trees, but do we really know how to use them in the garden design? Each plant has a particular shape and quality; when you look at a tree, think of it as a design element rather than as a trunk with branches, and think of flowers as color and texture.

SMALL TREES AND SHRUBS

Trees and shrubs are the permanent framework of the garden, whether in boxes or tubs or in the ground. Once in place, they are part of the total picture for many years. They are divided into two groups: deciduous trees that lose their leaves annually and evergreen trees that retain their leaves. There are two kinds of evergreens: the needle-leaf, cone-bearing shrubs and trees (conifers)—cedar, pine, spruce—and such broad-leaved evergreens as laurel and camellias. Because they hold color year round, evergreens are extremely popular.

There is a wide variation in foliage—the tiny leaves of heather, the bold leaves of evergreen magnolias, the large leaves of rhododendrons, and so forth. Use plants in terms of the texture and pattern of their foliage when planning the garden.

Deciduous plants are mostly used in cold climates and temperate zones because they add the needed interest of seasonal change and are indispensable displays when in bloom. Because deciduous plants shed their leaves in the winter, however, a garden of them has an airy structure and lacks mass and strength, so one should use evergreens with them.

49

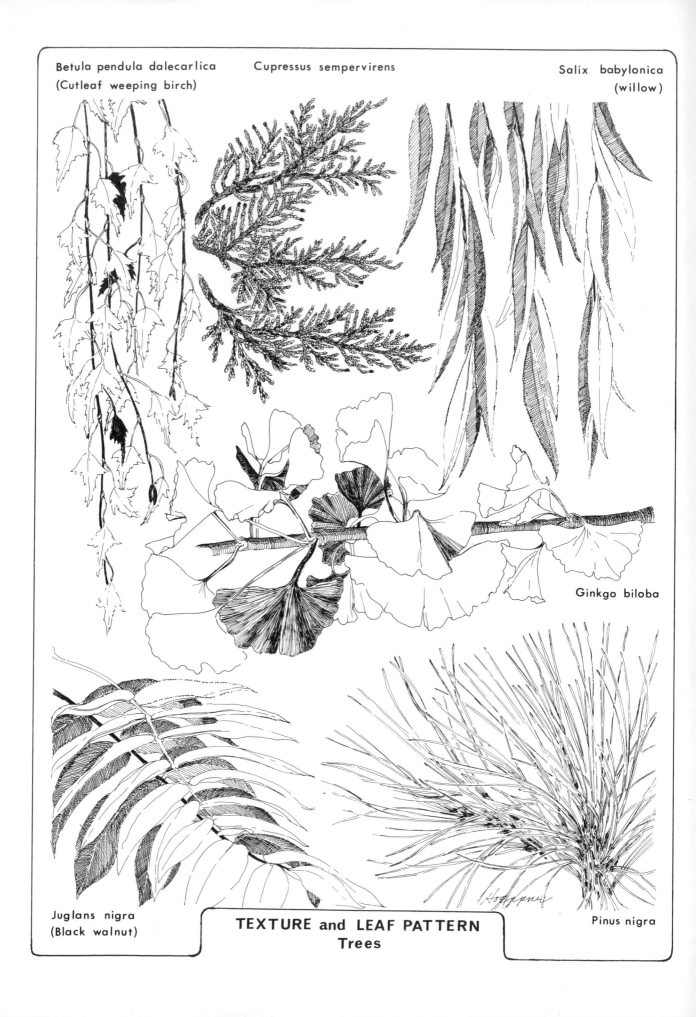

Betula pendula dalecarlica
(Cutleaf weeping birch)

Cupressus sempervirens

Salix babylonica
(willow)

Ginkgo biloba

Juglans nigra
(Black walnut)

TEXTURE and LEAF PATTERN
Trees

Pinus nigra

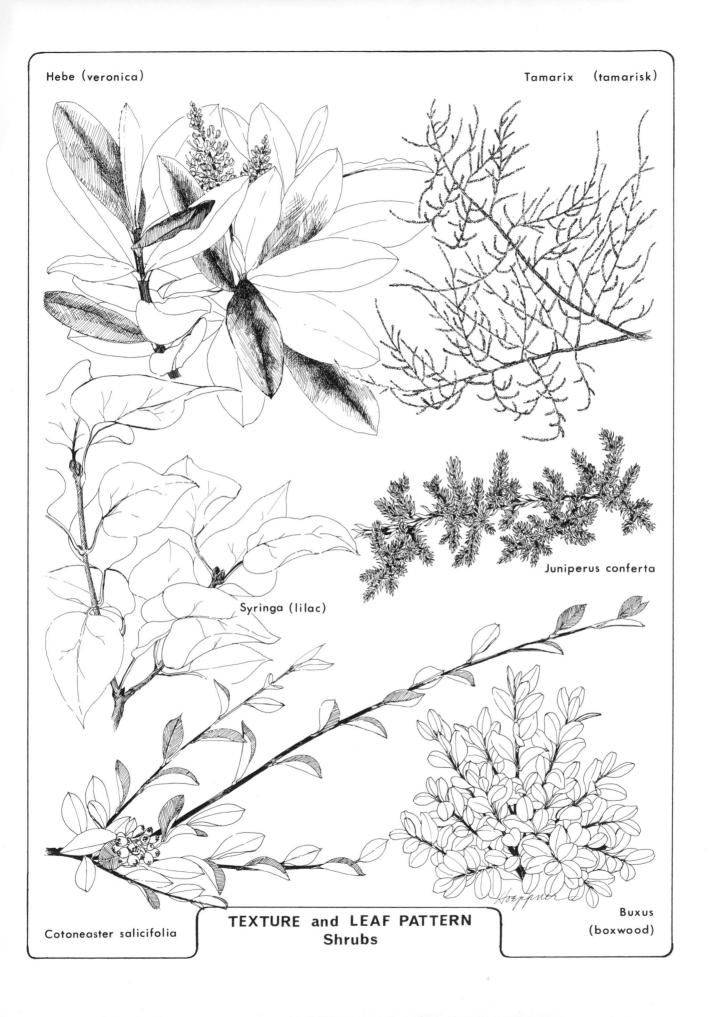

Hebe (veronica)

Tamarix (tamarisk)

Juniperus conferta

Syringa (lilac)

Cotoneaster salicifolia

TEXTURE and LEAF PATTERN
Shrubs

Buxus
(boxwood)

A plant's natural character is important in the overall plan; some grow in the shade and moisture and are dark green and lush. Others, such as desert plants, are generally pale green and sterile in appearance. Thus, try to approximate the natural growing conditions of garden plants so that they will be easy to maintain and look as if they belong to the scene. Trees are accents and form the garden's framework with shrubs massed around them. Perennials, annuals, biennials, and bulbs provide seasonal color and contrast.

Deciduous trees seem difficult to place in the landscape unless you think of them without their leaves. Then the line pattern of the branches can be used effectively. Some trees, like the weeping willows with their pendant branches, are good for vertical accents because they carry the eye downward. Learn the architectural qualities of trees—columnar, mushroom-topped, fan-shaped, canopy—and use them accordingly to create a balanced design. Imagine the pattern of the tree against a winter sky and use the lines of the tree—vertical, horizontal, pendant—to tie the landscape plan together.

Trees and shrubs are beautifully combined in this photo; the sculptural qualities of the trees are dominant, the shrubs a lesser accent in the background. Photo courtesy of Westinghouse Electric Company.

Leaf texture is used with infinite care in this landscape; large leaves, medium-sized foliage, and tiny leaves (lower left) create a feeling of movement and beauty. Photo by Roger Scharmer.

The coniferous evergreens are strong and dark and add contrast. Do not use too many, for they break up a garden plan and will give a crowded appearance on a small property. Evergreens generally have clearly defined trunks; they frequently are effective as foundation plantings or are placed near a building because the brick, stone, or concrete demands equal, heavy strength.

Broad-leaved evergreen shrubs are lovely in bloom, but select them for foliage because they bloom only about one month of the year. The leaves and branches give a definite pattern to the entire textured mass. Some have big, bold leaves and others bear delicate lacy foliage. Pay attention to the related sequence of foliage as you place plants. A large-leaved shrub needs a medium-leaved one next to it, followed by a small-leaved shrub, and ending with a tiny-leaved variety. Build up or down in relation to the leaf size—small, medium, or large—to achieve the rhythm that is part of a lovely garden. A stand of any one shrub is usually monotonous and overpowering. For an effective picture use shrubs with reference to leaf gradations.

Small trees with lacy foliage and large trees with bold leaves are perfectly married to make this landscape pleasing in all quarters. Very small-leaved foundation plantings complete the picture. Photo by Molly Adams.

Roses in a planter box are a colorful foil in this textured foliage scene. The combination of plants is highly pleasing. Note the bold-leaved plant at right to balance the overall effect. Photo by Clint Bryant.

Deciduous shrubs generally have somewhat soft, delicate foliage and are excellent behind perennials and annuals. Their leaves are akin to the soft texture of their flowers. When possible, use broad-leaved evergreens with their strong patterns and textures behind deciduous shrubs, so that there is a gradual change of textures as the eye views the scene. There is no rough break or jarring transition, but rather a smooth flow of plant material.

The following list should help you in your planning. This is by no means a complete list, but merely a sampling of the many small trees available. To determine if a plant will grow in your climate, ask your local nurseryman.

This is a predominantly green scene with bold dark green accents in the rear, lighter green, more fragile plantings in the foreground. Photo by Roger Scharmer.

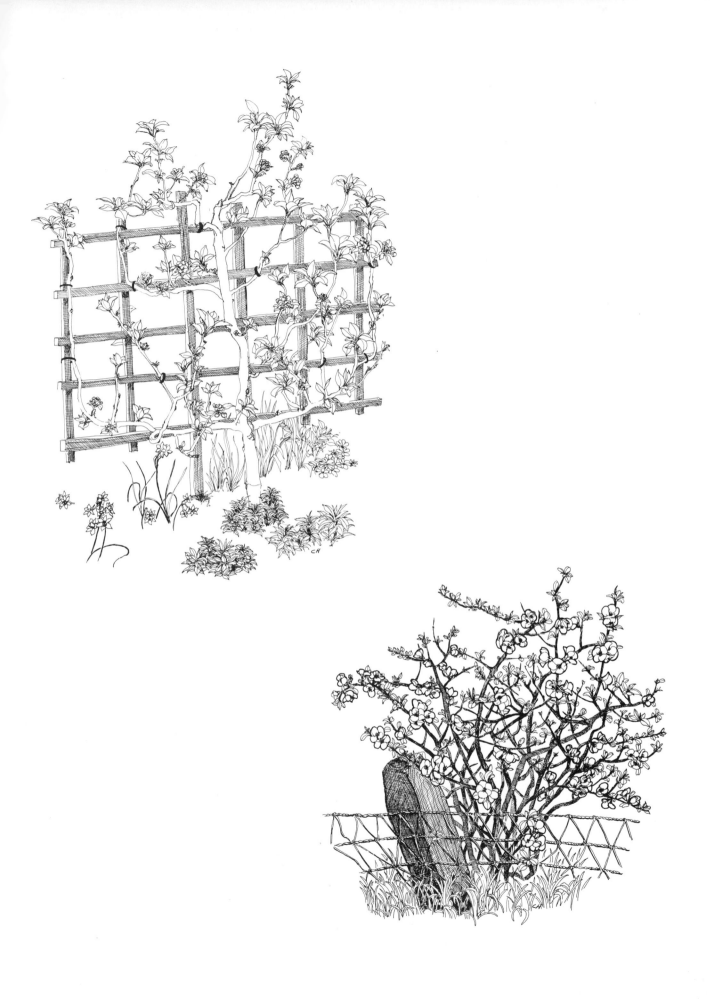

Small Trees:

Acer ginnala—Amur maple
A. palmatum—Japanese maple
Albizzia julibrissin—silk-tree
Amelanchier grandiflora—shadbush
Betula papyrifera—paper birch
B. pendula laciniata—cutleaf weeping birch
Cercis canadensis—redbud
Chionanthus virginica—fringe-tree
Cornus alternifolia—pagoda dogwood
C. florida—flowering dogwood
C. kousa—Chinese dogwood
C. nuttallii—Western flowering dogwood
Crataegus (various)—hawthorn
Davidia involucrata—dove-tree
Euonymus bungeanus—spindle-tree
E. europaea—spindle-tree
Gordonia alatamaha—Franklin tree
Halesia monticola—silver-bell tree
Koelreuteria paniculata—golden-rain tree
Laburnum anagyroides—golden-chain tree
Magnolia 'Dr. Merrill' hybrid
Magnolia soulangeana—saucer magnolia
M. stellata—starry magnolia
Malus (various)—flowering crabapple
Oxydendrum arboreum—sour-wood
Prunus (various)—flowering cherry, etc.
Robinia pseudoacacia "Fastigiata"—locust
Salix blanda—Wisconsin weeping willow
S. matsudana "Tortuosa"—corkscrew willow
Sophora japonica—Japanese pagoda tree
Sorbus (various)—mountain-ash
Stewartia pseudo-camellia—stewartia
Styrax japonica—storax
Syringa amurensis japonica—lilac tree
Wisteria sinensis—Chinese wisteria, tree form

(See Chapter 9 for plants for city conditions.)

6. Vines for Beauty and Privacy ✒

In the small garden, vines and trailers serve a dual purpose: they are decorative, and they can become a leafy green wall for privacy or shade. Properly selected with an eye on leaf texture and size, they can make a small area seem larger and also cover an unsightly wall or fence.

With contemporary architecture, which often uses bare expanses of walls and sometimes rather sterile lines, vines become an essential part of any good landscape plan. They are stellar decoration for screening walls or fences or blocking out an objectionable view. They fit into small spaces and can assume many shapes, and the flowering kinds are breathtaking in bloom.

There are numerous vines to use, some more effective in one area than another. Several offer fine flowers; others are valued for their rich texture or exquisite leaf patterns. Vines can become a highly ornamental part of the small garden, but they must be pruned and trained to a desired shape to create handsome compositions.

Some of the climbing vines, like clematis, bougainvillea, and morning glory, can become delightful screens of living color with proper care. Vines, such as stephanotis, wisteria, and sweet pea, have a dainty loveliness about them and a fragile quality that is often necessary to soften harsh garden walls and house lines. And many vines—euonymus, bittersweet, pyracantha—have colorful winter berries that are indispensable in the snow landscape.

A SUITABLE SUPPORT
Many vines climb by means of twining stems that need support;

This small area depends on the vines on the house wall for its appealing look.
G. Woodard photo.

others have tendrils or discs. Some vines have leaflike appendages that act as tendrils, grasping the object on which they grow. Other plants, like jasmine, have long slender arching stems and need support, and some, such as ivy geranium and trailing lantana, are prostrate in growth. Along with growth habit, vines may be open to delicate or heavy with masses of foliage. Several varieties grow rapidly in a few months, but others take years to fill a space. Select vines carefully; do not choose them indiscriminately or constant care may be needed.

Few vines will look good or thrive without a support—a trellis, wood grid, wall; they become vagrant and lose their vine characteristics. If there is no wall, a support must be furnished that is sturdy enough to hold the weight of the vine. Metal frame lattices are good,

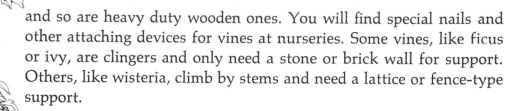

and so are heavy duty wooden ones. You will find special nails and other attaching devices for vines at nurseries. Some vines, like ficus or ivy, are clingers and only need a stone or brick wall for support. Others, like wisteria, climb by stems and need a lattice or fence-type support.

VINES AS GARDEN PLANTS

Many vines are annuals or are treated as annuals in the northern part of the United States. They are showy for a long time in summer and can be started in tubs, if desired, in early spring. In northern locations start the plants indoors in a warm sunny place about eight weeks before the last frost-free days by putting seeds into five-inch-diameter pots. When warm weather starts, place the pots outside. A perennial vine is a plant that lasts for many years, old roots sprouting new growth each spring. They are easily grown once established, but like all vines they will need periodic pruning and shaping.

Some plants can grow untended; vines cannot. These green traceries must be kept in bounds by pruning and by intelligent shaping. A vine, especially in a small garden, that is not meticulously trained becomes an eyesore. Do not let the plant get so lush that it gets tangled in its own growth.

Water and good soil are necessary requirements of course, but most vines will tolerate some neglect, other than the pruning aspect.

For vines growing on a flat surface like a wall or fence, selection of suitable varieties with handsome leaves is essential. Pay attention to leaf size and texture; fine small leaves clothe a wall handsomely and, to some extent, larger-leaved species can be used too. For vines trained overhead or on a trellis, leaf pattern is not as important; flowers are perhaps more desirable here, for a living ceiling of color is dramatic indeed and can make the small garden a veritable wonderland.

Trailing sweet peas soften the sharp edges of this deck garden. Photo by author.

Flowering vines help beautify this patio; this is lavender trumpet vine. Photo courtesy of California Assocation of Nurserymen.

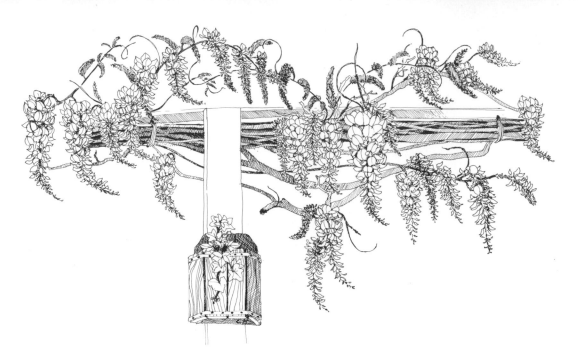

Plant woody vines in a deep planting hole to a depth of about three to four feet, so that the roots will have ample growing space. Replace the dug-out soil with good topsoil, but do not include manure or fertilizers that may burn the plants. When in place, tamp the earth gently around the collar of the plant, so that air pockets will not form. Water thoroughly and deeply, and for the first few weeks give the plant some extra attention. (This merely means watching it to see that it is getting started.) Once established, it can have routine care.

Choose vines carefully, provide suitable supports, and keep them well trained, and you will be amazed at what they can do for the garden. However, they are essentially outlaws and will, if not stopped, grow over their neighbor plants. Remember too that once in a place against a wall, a vine is difficult to remove in order to paint that wall, so choose plants accordingly.

VINES

BOTANICAL AND COMMON NAME	MINIMUM NIGHT TEMPERATURE	GENERAL DESCRIPTION	SUN OR SHADE	REMARKS
Akebia quinata (fiveleaf akebia)	−20° to −10°F.	Vigorous twiner with fragrant small flowers	Sun or partial shade	Needs support; prune in fall or early spring
Allamanda cathartica	Tender	Dense with heavy stems, lovely tubular flowers	Sun	Prune annually in spring
Ampelopsis brevipedunculata (porcelain ampelopsis) (blueberry climber)	−20° to −10°F.	Strong grower with dense leaves	Sun or shade	Prune in early spring
Antigonon leptopsus (coral vine) (queen's wreath)	Tender	Excellent as screen	Sun	Needs light support; prune hard after bloom
Aristolochia durior (Dutchman's pipe)	−20° to −10°F.	Big twiner with mammoth leaves	Sun or shade	Needs sturdy support; prune in spring or summer
Celastrus scandens (American bitter-sweet)	−50° to −35°F.	Light green leaves with red berries	Sun or shade	Prune in early spring before growth starts
Clematis armandi (evergreen clematis)	5° to 10°F.	Lovely flowers and foliage, many colors	Sun	Needs support; prune lightly after bloom
Clytostoma (*Bignonia capreolata*) (cross vine) (trumpet vine)	−5° to 5°F.	Orange flowers	Sun or shade	Thin out weak branches in spring; clings by discs
Doxantha unguis-cati	10° to 20°F.	Dark green leaves with yellow blooms	Sun	Needs no support; prune hard after bloom
Euonymus fortunei (wintercreeper)	−35° to −20°F.	Shiny leathery leaves, orange berries in fall	Sun or shade	Needs support; prune in early spring

BOTANICAL AND COMMON NAME	MINIMUM NIGHT TEMPERATURE	GENERAL DESCRIPTION	SUN OR SHADE	REMARKS
Fatshedera lizei	20° to 30°F.	Grown for handsome foliage	Shade	No pruning needed
Ficus pumila (repens) (creeping fig)	20° to 30°F.	Small heart-shaped leaves	Partial shade	Thin plant in late fall or early spring
Gelsemium sempervirens (Carolina jessamine)	Tender	Fragrant yellow flowers	Sun or partial shade	Needs support; thin plant immediately after bloom
Hedera helix (English ivy)	−10 to −5°F.	Scalloped neat leaves, many varieties	Shade	Prune and thin in early spring
Hydrangea petiolaris (climbing hydrangea)	−20° to −10°F.	Heads of snowy flowers	Sun or partial shade	Thin and prune in winter or early spring
Ipomoea purpurea (Morning glory) (Convolvulus)	Tender	White, blue, purple, pink, or red flowers	Sun	Bloom until frost
Jasminum nudiflorum (winter jasmine)	−10 to −5°F.	Yellow flowers	Sun or shade	Needs strong support; thin and shape annually after bloom
J. officinale (white jasmine)	5° to 10°F.	Showy dark green leaves with white flowers	Sun or shade	Provide strong support; thin and shape after bloom
Kadsura japonica (scarlet kadsura)	5° to 10°F.	Bright red berries in fall	Sun	Provide support; prune annually in early spring
Lonicera caprifolium (sweet honeysuckle)	−10° to −5°F.	White or yellow trumpet flowers	Sun	Prune in fall or spring
L. hildebrandiana (Burmese honey-suckle)	20° to 30°F.	Shiny dark green leaves	Sun or partial shade	Needs support; prune in late fall

BOTANICAL AND COMMON NAME	MINIMUM NIGHT TEMPERATURE	GENERAL DESCRIPTION	SUN OR SHADE	REMARKS
L. japonica 'Halliana' (Hall's honeysuckle) (Japanese honey-suckle)	−20° to −10°F.	Deep green leaves, bronze in fall	Sun or shade	Provide support; prune annually in fall and spring
Mandevilla suaveolens (laxa) (Chilean jasmine)	20° to 30°F.	Heart-shaped leaves and flowers	Sun	Trim and cut back lightly in fall; remove seed pods as they form
Parthenocissus quinquefolia (Virginia creeper) (American ivy)	−35° to −20°F.	Scarlet leaves in fall	Sun or shade	Prune in early spring
Passiflora caerulea (passion flower)	5° to 10°F.	Spectacular flowers	Sun	Needs support; prune hard annually in fall or early spring
Phaseolus coccineus (scarlet runner)	Tender	Bright red flowers	Sun	Renew each spring
Plumbago capensis (plumbago)	20° to 30°F.	Blue flowers	Sun	Prune some-what in spring
Pueraria thunbergiana (Kudzu vine)	−5° to 5°F.	Purple flowers	Sun or partial shade	Provide sturdy support; cut back hard annually in fall
Rosa (rambler rose)	−10° to −5°F.	Many varieties	Sun	Needs support; prune out dead wood, shorten long shoots, and cut laterals back to two nodes in spring or early summer after bloom
Smilax rotundifolia (horsebriar)	−20° to −10°F.	Good green foliage	Sun or shade	Needs no support; prune hard annually any time

BOTANICAL AND COMMON NAME	MINIMUM NIGHT TEMPERATURE	GENERAL DESCRIPTION	SUN OR SHADE	REMARKS
Trachelospermum jasminoides (star jasmine)	20° to 30°F.	Dark green leaves with small white flowers	Partial shade	Provide heavy support; prune very lightly in fall
Vitis coignetiae (glory grape)	−10° to 5°F.	Colorful autumn leaves	Sun or partial shade	Needs sturdy support; prune annually in fall or spring
Wisteria floribunda (Japanese wisteria)	−20° to −10°F.	Violet blue flowers	Sun	Provide support; prune annually once mature to shorten long branches after bloom or in winter; pinch back branches first year

sinensis ✓

LIST OF VINES

Twining Vines:

Akebia quinata (fiveleaf akebia)
Aristolochia durior (Dutchman's pipe)
Celastrus species (bittersweet)
Mandevilla suaveolens (Chilean jasmine)
Smilax rotundifolia (horsebriar)
Trachelospermum jasminoides (star jasmine)
Wisteria floribunda (Japanese wisteria)

Climbing Vines:

Ampelopsis species
Bignonia capreolata (cross vine)
Clematis species
Doxantha unguis-cati
Parthenocissus quinquefolia (Virginia creeper)
Passiflora species (passion flower)
Vitis coignetiae (glory grape)

Rapid-Growing Vines:

Akebia quinata (fiveleaf akebia)
Ampelopsis aconitifolia
Aristolochia durior (Dutchman's pipe)
Bignonia capreolata (cross vine)
Clematis species
Doxantha unguis-cati
Ficus pumila (creeping fig)
Hedera helix (English ivy)
Lonicera species (honeysuckle)
Trachelospermum jasminoides (star jasmine)
Vitis coignetiae (glory grape)
Wisteria floribunda (Japanese wisteria)
W. sinensis (Chinese wisteria)

Vines for Flowers:

Bignonia capreolata (cross vine)
Clematis
Hydrangea petiolaris (climbing hydrangea)
Mandevilla suaveolens (Chilean jasmine)
Passiflora caerulea (passion flower)
Plumbago capensis (plumbago)
Rosa (rambler rose)
Trachelospermum jasminoides (star jasmine)
Wisteria floribunda (Japanese wisteria)

Vines for Colorful Fruit:

Celastrus scandens (American bittersweet)
Euonymus fortunei (winter creeper)
Kadsura japonica (scarlet kadsura)
Smilax rotundifolia (horsebriar)

7. The Flower Garden (Annuals and Perennials) ✍

Garden flowers are an essential part of the outdoor scene, but too often they *are* the garden. Remember that no matter how beautiful flowers may appear in catalogs and pictures, herbaceous plants—perennials, annuals, and biennials—are only part of the picture. Do not stress them too much or your garden will become more of a chore than a charm.

Herbaceous plants die down to the ground after their flowering time, and they do not form a permanent woody growth. They are in no way a structural design element. Plan your garden first the way you want it without flowers; then add the perennials and annuals. Use flowers only for what they are—seasonal color.

The Planting Plan

Use herbaceous plants for flowering seasons only, and, as mentioned, remember that they do not make a year-round garden. First, plant without them; put in the structure of shrubs and trees, so that flowers grown for seasonal accent will be suitably framed all year and will not be missed when they are out of bloom.

For maximum effect, set flowers in curves and frame them with shrub groups, for flowers need a good background to be really effective. With a plain background of sky or fence you will see nothing but empty spaces. Masses of shrubs will show off the blooms and still provide an attractive background. Plant flowers in sweeping arcs and curves; strive for a mass of concentrated color in one area rather than a mixed planting of many colors.

The spring, summer, or fall flower garden placed in one area has

72

been greatly recommended by many gardeners. It is beautiful, but generally it requires too much work for the average homeowner and certainly demands utmost arranging skill to be successful.

Keep your flower garden simple, and don't expect continuous color from spring to fall. If a mass of flowers year-round is your goal, use one area for spring bloom, another for summer, and still another for fall. However, because most properties today are small, this is a difficult gardening method.

If you have only one place for flowers, grow mostly perennials and bulbs interplanted with shrubs. Do not rely too much on annuals with short bloom seasons; select the ones that provide color all summer (petunias or snapdragons, for example). Do not put too many varieties in a small area or crowd too great a color range into it. The effect will be a spotty picture.

Consider the shape of flowers as you plant; some are round-headed, others are spikes. The spike forms are sharp accent points in the garden, so do not use too many of them. Place a mass of them in one area, and balance them with another area of round-headed flowers. Also consider the size of the flower. Do not put tiny blooms next to giants or the scale of the arrangement will be disrupted. Arrange gradual changes from tiny to small to medium to large flowers, or vice versa.

With annuals and perennials, plan a concentrated mass or drift. You want to create free-form, curving masses of color; only with rare exceptions plant in a straight line or row. Be bold and imaginative with herbaceous plants, as straight lines of flowers are not attractive.

73

Flower gardening is more working with color than with flowers. A line of blue along a flower bed is not effective in the landscape, but a concentrated mass of blue is indeed dramatic. And even though a colored square or rectangle on a broad green canvas can be handsome in some situations, curved forms are more pleasing because they suggest movement, which is the basis of putting flowers in free-form patterns or drifts. These forms can take many shapes, but basically they should follow these principles:

1. Use bold curves in small areas.
2. The height of the planting should have some relation to the width of the bed.
3. Do not plan outcurves at lot corners; there you want to create space.
4. Use heavy and high plantings in the curve and lighter plantings in the bays.

A mass of daffodils surrounds a tree, a lovely frame for the garden. Never use sparse plantings of flowers; group them for a mass display. Photo courtesy of Westinghouse Electric Company.

A curving drift of petunias provides show and drama in a landscape; the graceful elliptical curve of flowers is repeated in the rear of the photo. Photo courtesy of George Ball Seed Company.

The flower garden can be almost any shape and width, but remember that you have to get to the flowers at the back without stepping over those in the front. (The width must not exceed thirty inches.) Put tall flowers at the rear, medium-sized ones in the middle, and the smallest growers up front. Intersperse them with larger clumps of medium-sized varieties in the background and foreground to relieve monotony.

Annuals and biennials are generally raised from seed; perennials are best bought as seedlings at nurseries.

Color and Its Effect
When you are working with flower color, know the elements of value, hue, and intensity so that you can use flowers intelligently.

Masses of flowers are used here to create a showy display; one group runs into the other to provide constant eye interest. Photo by Molly Adams.

Value is the lightness and darkness of a color. Hue is the gradation or actual color—red or orange separated by the warm colors of yellow, orange, scarlet, or crimson, for example. (The cool hues include blue, green, purple, and their derivatives.) There are several shades of one color, from pale to dark; this difference in tones is the intensity of a color.

To use color effectively, first decide where there is to be light or dark color, and employ different shades in rhythmic steps to achieve a harmonious effect—say, pale pink, medium pink, and dark or intense pink. If you want a dark color to predominate, have dark-colored flowers; to stress a light color, use light-colored flowers.

When you work with warm colors, for example, begin with red, followed by orange red, orange, pale orange, orange yellow, pale yellow, beige, and ending with white. Follow a very gradual sequence rather than switching from orange to white and creating a jarring effect. A mono-chromatic color scheme is the most effective way to display flowers in the garden. With cool colors start with blue and finish with purple, again building up gradually rather than abruptly.

CULTURE

With few exceptions, annuals, perennials, and biennials will need as much sunlight as they can get. And although soil requirements vary, if drainage is good, most plants will thrive regardless. For maximum growth provide a neutral soil that is reasonably light in texture and a good amount of humus.

If you want lots of flowers, always keep the flower bed evenly moist. Herbaceous plants can take great quantities of water; the soil should never be dry. The key to a lush and colorful flower garden is to water plants thoroughly and deeply, especially on hot, sunny days. Sometimes in August I sprinkle plants from early morning to noon.

Keep the soil weeded; mulching it will save much work (see Chapter 12). Feed annuals and perennials a few weeks after they are planted and then at monthly inter   . Established perennials need feeding as soon as growth start   ing and again at four- to six-week intervals until they blo

The following is a mere s   ng of flowers. We have not included varieties because of space, but all suppliers list special varieties of outstanding color; consult nursery catalogs for their descriptions.

PERENNIALS AND BIENNIALS

Achillea ptarmica (yarrow or sneezewort)—white flowers in summer or fall; grows to 18 inches

Althaea rosea (hollyhock)—most colors except true blue and green; lovely autumn flowers; grows to 10 feet

Anchusa capensis (summer forget-me-not)—pure bright blue blooms in early summer; grows to 18 inches; needs sunlight or light shade.

Anemone japonica (Japanese anemone)—white, pink, or rose flowers in fall; grows to 48 inches; needs sunlight or light shade

Anthemis tinctoria (golden Marguerite)—yellow flowers in summer or fall; grows to 36 inches

Arabis caucasica (wall rockcress)—white flowers in early spring; grows to 10 inches; needs sunlight or light shade

Artemisia albula (wormwood)—silvery gray blooms in summer and fall; grows to 48 inches

Asclepias tuberosa (butterfly weed)—orange flowers in summer; grows to 36 inches

Aster novae-angliae (New England aster)—mainly blue and purple flowers in fall; grows to 5 feet

Begonia semperflorens (wax begonia)—white, pink, and deep rose flowers all summer; grows to 18 inches; needs sunlight or shade

Bergenia cordifolia (heartleaf bergenia)—white or rose flowers in early summer; grows to 18 inches; needs sunlight or light shade

Campanula persicifolia (willow bellflower)—white or blue flowers in summer; grows to 36 inches

Chrysanthemum coccineum (pyrethrum or painted daisy)—white, pink, or red blooms in early summer; grows to 36 inches

C. maximum (Shasta daisy)—white flowers in summer and fall; grows to 48 inches

Coreopsis grandiflora (tick-seed)—golden yellow flowers in summer; grows to 36 inches

Delphinium hybrid (Connecticut Yankee)—blue, violet, or white flowers in early summer; grows to 36 inches

Dianthus barbatus (sweet William)—white, pink, red, or rose flowers, zoned and edged, in early summer; grows to 24 inches; needs sunlight or light shade

Dicentra spectabilis (bleeding-heart)—white, pink, or rose flowers in spring; grows to 36 inches; needs light shade

Digitalis purpurea (common foxglove)—mixed colors, marked and spotted; blooms in early summer; grows to 30 inches; needs sunlight or partial shade

Epimedium grandiflorum (bishop's hat)—red and violet flowers in summer; grows to 12 inches; needs light shade

Felicia amelloides (blue Marguerite)—blue flowers in spring and summer; grows to 24 inches

Gentiana asclepiadea (willow gentian)—blue to violet flowers in late summer; grows to 24 inches; needs light shade

Even a single clump of flowers (if massed) can be effective in a garden. Here peonies frame an entrance. Photo by Molly Adams.

Gypsophila paniculata (baby's breath)—white flowers all summer; grows to 36 inches

Helianthus decapetalus multiflorus (sunflower)—yellow flowers in summer; grows to 48 inches

Hemerocallis (various; day lily)—all colors but blue, green, violet, and true red; blooms in spring and summer; grows to 6 feet; needs sunlight or light shade

Heuchera sanguinea (coral bells)—red, pink, and white flowers in early summer; grows to 18 inches; needs sunlight or light shade

Iberis sempervirens (evergreen candytuft)—white flowers in early spring to summer; grows to 12 inches

Iris cristata (crested iris)—lavender and light blue flowers in spring; grows to 8 inches; needs light shade

I. kaempferi (Japanese iris)—purple, violet, pink, rose, red, and white flowers in spring and early summer; grows to 48 inches; needs sunlight or light shade

Lilium (various; lily)—white, pink, yellow, gold, and bicolor flowers in early summer; grows to 7 feet; needs sunlight or light shade

Linum perenne (blue flax)—sky-blue flowers in summer; grows to 24 inches

Lobelia cardinalis (cardinal flower)—red flowers in late summer; grows to 36 inches

Lythrum (various)—rose to purple flowers in summer; grows to 5 feet; needs sunlight or light shade

Mertensia virginica (Virginia bluebells or cowslip)—bicolor blue blooms in early spring; grows to 18 inches; needs light shade

Monarda didyma (bee-balm)—white, pink, and scarlet red flowers in summer and fall; grows to 36 inches

Papaver orientale (Oriental poppy)—pink, white, scarlet, or salmon flowers in early summer; grows to 48 inches

Pentstemon (various; beard-tongue)—blue, pink, and crimson flowers, mostly bicolors, in summer and fall; grows to 36 inches

Phlox paniculata (summer perennial phlox)—pink, purple, rose, white, orange, and red flowers in late summer to fall; grows to 5 feet

Physostegia virginiana (false dragonhead)—white and rose bicolors; blooms mid to late summer; grows to 5 feet

Polygonatum multiflorum (Solomon's seal)—white flowers in spring; grows to 12 inches; needs sunlight or shade

Primula (primrose)—blooms in bicolors of blue, red, and yellow in late spring; grows to 14 inches

Rudbeckia hirta (black-eyed Susan)—yellow, pink, orange, and white flowers in summer; grows to 48 inches

Scabiosa caucasica (pincushion flower)—white, blue, and purple flowers in summer and fall; grows to 30 inches

Solidago (goldenrod)—yellow flowers in summer; grows to 24 inches; needs sunlight or light shade

Tritoma (kniphofia; torch lily)—cream, white, yellow, and orange flowers in early summer; grows to 6 feet

Viola cornuta (tufted pansy)—purple flowers, but newer varieties in many colors; blooms in spring and fall; grows to 8 inches; needs light shade

ANNUALS

Ageratum houstonianum (blue blazer)—blue flowers in summer and fall; grows to 12 inches

Amaranthus tricolor (Joseph's coat)—bronze green crown, foliage marked cream and red; blooms in summer; grows to 7 feet

Antirrhinum majus (common or large snapdragon)—large choice of colors and flower form; blooms in late spring and fall, and in summer where cool; grows to 48 inches

Begonia semperflorens (wax begonia)—white, pink, and deep rose flowers all summer; grows to 18 inches; needs sunlight or shade

This small flower garden is brimming with color; the plants are delphiniums, phlox, and veronica. Photo by Molly Adams.

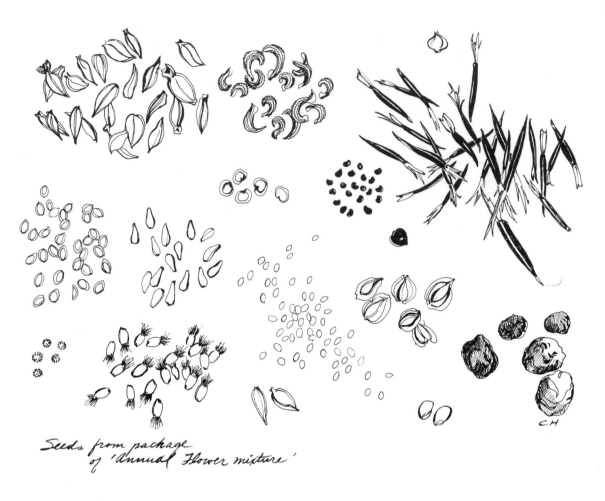

Seeds from package of 'Annual Flower mixture'

Calendula officinalis (calendula or pot marigold)—cream, yellow, orange, and apricot flowers in winter where mild, late spring elsewhere; grows to 24 inches

Centaurea cyanus (bachelor's button or cornflower)—blue, pink, wine, and white flowers in spring where mild, summer elsewhere; grows to 30 inches

Clarkia unguiculata (mountain garland)—white, pink, rose, crimson, purple, and salmon blooms; flowers in late spring to early summer; grows to 36 inches

Cosmos bipinnatus (cosmos)—white, pink lavender, rose, and purple flowers all summer; grows to 6 feet

Delphinium ajacis (rocket larkspur)—blue, pink, lavender, rose, salmon, carmine, and white flowers in late spring to early summer; grows to 5 feet

Eschscholtzia californica (California poppy)—gold, yellow, and orange; 'Mission Bell' varieties include pink and rose flowers in winter, and in spring in mild climates; grows to 24 inches

82

Gomphrena globosa (globe amaranth, bachelor's button)—white, crimson, violet, dull gold flowers all summer; heat-resistant; grows to 36 inches

Helianthus annuus (common garden sunflower)—yellow and mahogany bicolors or yellow with black centers; blooms in summer; grows to 120 inches or more

Iberis amara (rocket candytuft)—white flowers in late spring; grows to 20 inches

Impatiens balsamina (garden balsam)—white, pink, rose, and red flowers in summer to fall; grows to 30 inches; needs light shade, sunlight where cool

Lathyrus odoratus (winter-flowering sweet pea)—mixed or separate colors, except yellow, orange, and green; blooms in late winter where mild; not heat-resistant; grows to 72 inches

Linum grandiflorum (flowering flax)—scarlet to deep red or rose flowers in late spring and fall; grows to 18 inches

Lobularia maritima (sweet alyssum)—white, purple, lavender, and rosy pink flowers; blooms year-round where mild, spring to fall elsewhere; grows to 8 inches

Mathiola incana (stock)—white, cream, yellow, pink, rose, crimson, red, and purple flowers in winters where mild, late spring elsewhere; grows to 36 inches

Molucella laevis (shell flower)—green, bell-like bracts resembling flowers; blooms in summer; grows to 30 inches

Nemesia strumosa (nemesia)—all colors but green; blooms in spring where mild, early summer elsewhere; grows to 18 inches

Nigella damascena (love-in-a-mist)—blue, white, and rose-pink flowers in summer; grows to 30 inches

Petunia hybrids—all colors except true blue, yellow, and orange; blooms summer and fall; grows to 18 inches

Physalis alkekengi (Chinese lantern plant)—white flowers, orange bracts; blooms in late summer; grows to 24 inches; needs sunlight or shade

Reseda odorata (common mignonette)—greenish brown clusters; blooms in late spring until fall; grows to 18 inches

Salpiglossis sinuata (painted-tongue)—flowers have bizarre patterns of red, orange, yellow, pink, and purple; blooms in early summer; grows to 36 inches

Scabiosa atropurpurea (sweet scabious)—purple, blue, mahogany, white, and rose flowers in spring; grows to 36 inches

Tagetes erecta (hybrids and species; African or Aztec marigold)—mostly yellow, tangerine, and gold flowers; blooms all summer except where hot; grows to 48 inches

T. tenuifolia signata (signet marigold)—small, yellow orange flowers; blooms all summer except where quite hot; grows to 24 inches

Tropaeolum majus (garden nasturtium)—white, pink, crimson, orange, maroon, and yellow flowers in spring and fall, summer where cool; grows to 18 inches, and some spread vigorously; needs sunlight or shade

Vinca roseus (Madagascar periwinkle)—white and pink flowers, some with contrasting eye; blooms in summer until early fall; grows to 24 inches

Viola tricolor v. 'Hortensis' (pansy)—"faces" in white, yellow, purple, rose, mahogany, violet, and apricot; blooms in spring and fall, winter where mild; grows to 8 inches

8. Container Plants for Small Gardens ✐

Container gardening is an easy way to create a small garden in a weekend: a plant is put within the confines of a container and placed where you want it for display, and because it is one area it can be watered easily.

The beauty, ease, and practicability of this kind of gardening cannot be ignored. This is instant color for a small garden, and there is no need to wait for plants to grow or to be concerned if the soil around the house (especially in city gardens) will not support plants. Almost any kind of plant—tree, shrub, flowering kind—can be grown in a tub or box, temporarily or permanently. Some plants, such as camellias and azaleas, do better in a box than in the ground, and varieties like the Bonanza peach and nectarine are especially bred for tub growing.

For a long time the standard plant container was the terra-cotta pot with a maximum size of sixteen inches in diameter but today there are many pots, tubs, and boxes to decorate the outdoors.

CONTAINERS
Because there are so many containers, it is wise to select them carefully with some idea of where they will be used, so that they will blend in with the setting. Here is a list of available containers:

The standard clay pot is now offered in many variations:

The *Italian type* has a modified border to a tightlipped detail and is simple and good looking. Some have round edges, while others are beveled or rimless, ranging from 12 to 24 inches in diameter.

This container garden is for beauty and accent in a small yard. Photo courtesy of Potted Plant Information Center.

Venetian pots are barrel-shapped with a concentric band design pressed into the sides. Somewhat formal in appearance, they come in 8- to 20-inch diameter sizes.

Spanish pots have outward slopping sides and flared lips and come in 8- to 12-inch diameter sizes. They have heavier walls than conventional pots and make good general containers for many plants.

Cylindrical pots, a recent innovation, are a departure from the traditional tapered design because they are perfectly straight from top to bottom. They come in three sizes with a maximum 14-inch diameter.

Bulb pans or *seed bowls* are generally less than half as wide as they are high. These shallow containers look like deep saucers, but have drain holes. They are available in 6- to 12-inch diameter sizes.

The *Azalea* or *fern pot* is a squatty container formerly sold in only a few sizes. It is three-quarters as high as it is wide, and it is in better proportion to most plants than conventional pots.

86

Three-legged pots are another recent offering that brings the bowl shape to the garden. They range in size from 8 to 20 inches in diameter.

Donkey or *chicken containers* are novelty pots with pockets for soil. *Strawberry jars* in various sizes are also offered at nurseries.

Plastic pots are lightweight and come in many sizes and colors, in round or square shapes. They are easy to clean and hold water longer than terra-cotta pots, so the plants require less frequent watering—an advantage to some gardeners. They are not suitable for large plants because they have a tendency to tip over. Most plastic pots are opaque, but there are some in small sizes (to 10 inches in diameter) that are translucent; however, I hardly find these attractive, as roots can be seen through them.

An intimate garden depends on container plants for seasonal color; note the handsome pineapple urn. Photo by Roger Scharmer.

Tubs and Boxes

Tubs may be round, square, or hexagonal in shape. Tubs made of suitable wood (redwood or cypress, for example) resist decay; otherwise, wooden tubs need a preservative coating. Stone or concrete tubs are ornamental, but are very heavy when filled with soil. Available in several sizes, tapered stone bowls are especially pretty with petunias or marigolds, and vegetables, herbs, and bulbs are all suitable choices, when tub grown, for the small garden.

Wooden boxes are necessary for most trees and shrubs because the largest tub does not hold enough soil or carry enough visual weight to balance a tree. Some boxes are perfect cubes, others a low cube. Some are detailed; others are plain.

Hanging baskets and self-watering containers complete the assortment of containers. No doubt more new designs and materials will be introduced in the future.

CARING FOR CONTAINER PLANTS

Soil

A good soil is important for all plants and especially for plants in tubs, pots, and boxes, which spend their lives in a confined space. Here are some basic soils I use:

For most plants:
2 parts garden loam
1 part sand
1 part leafmold
1 teaspoon bonemeal for an 8-inch pot

For begonias and ferns:
2 parts garden loam
2 parts sand
2 parts leafmold

For bulbs:
2 parts garden loam
1 part sand
1 part leafmold

For cacti and succulents:
2 parts garden loam
2 parts sand
1 part leafmold
handful of limestone for an 8-inch pot

For bromeliads and orchids:
1 part medium-grade fir bark
1 part chopped osmunda

POTTING

To pot a plant, place sufficient drainage material in the bottom of the container, so that excess water drains away quickly. (Use broken pieces of pots or some crushed stone.) Spread a layer of soil over the stones, about three inches deep for a sixteen-inch diameter container. Remove the plant to be potted from its original container. Do not pull or tug it loose; try to tease it out by gently juggling it back and forth. Center the plant on the bed of soil, and fill in around it with fresh soil, pressing down with your fingers or a blunt-edged piece of wood to eliminate air pockets. Do not press the soil tightly in place, but be sure it is firm. Add more soil until the pot is filled to within an inch of the rim. Water thoroughly, and place in a partially shaded area for a few days; then move it to its permanent place.

Be sure the size of the plant is in proportion to the container. A small plant will not be attractive in a large pot, and unused portions of the soil are liable to become waterlogged, harming the plant. A big plant in a small pot is hardly handsome and in most cases does not grow well.

WATERING

Container plants exposed to the elements dry out more quickly than plants in the ground. Of course, watering them depends on rainfall, the size of the container (large ones dry out more slowly than small ones), and the type of box or tub used. Glazed pots without drainage holes—urns and jugs—need careful watering to avoid a stagnant soil. Wooden tubs and boxes dry out slowly, and metal containers stay wet for many days.

When you water, really soak the plant. Sparse watering results in

Even a few container plants heighten an area. A hanging basket is at eye level with two floor plants. Photo by Roger Scharmer.

pockets of the soil becoming wet and eventually waterlogged. Water should run freely out of the drainage hole. A good rule is to water plants thoroughly and then allow them to become somewhat dry before watering them again. Occasionally hose down the foliage to flush out hidden insects in the leaf axils and veins. Because large plants are difficult to move to the water source, use a damp cloth to wipe their leaves.

FEEDING

Container plants need feeding. Use a commercial soluble fertilizer 10-10-5 (contents marked on bottle) mixed weaker than the direc-

90

tions on the bottle indicate, but use it more often. Avoid a set schedule for feeding plants. In general, large plants in containers eighteen to thirty-six inches in diameter will need feeding about four times in the summer, and those in smaller pots about once a month during the growing season. Do not feed ailing plants or newly potted ones. Do not feed at all in winter, but light solutions can be given once in early spring and once in fall.

PLANTS TO GROW

There is no end to the kinds of plants that can be grown in a tub or box. Small trees are always desirable for the patio or terrace, and shrubs are essential to make a setting attractive. Plants grown to tree

Container plants frame this entry; standard clay pots are used with a Venetian pot. Photo by Roger Scharmer.

form (standards) and espaliers (plants shaped against a wall) are touches of elegance that make an area unique.

Large pots filled with soil weigh a great deal; make provisions for moving them. Commercial dollies are available at nurseries, or make your own moving devices: use two by four boards with casters under them.

Small trees are basic container subjects that offer some shade and provide visual background. The relationship of the tree and its tub must be considered. For example, a four-foot tree would be minimum for a twenty-four-inch diameter container; it gives a satisfying balance. Square or rectangular boxes are best for trees with bold foliage, and a lacy-leaved Japanese maple looks best in the graceful outlines of a round container.

Small trees at nurseries come in five-, ten-, or fifteen-gallon cans. Decide whether you want a fast-growing or a slow-growing kind. If you are not in a temperate, year-round climate, consider where the tree will go in the winter. Some can be placed in a sunny window, others in an unheated but not freezing garage or porch; and even a basement with a little light is a place to store some plants.

In climates with severe winters, and where there is no indoor space for plants, select hardy trees and shrubs. The degree of hardiness is difficult to determine, and each section of the country has its own definition; however, there are certain plants that are considered hardy where temperatures go well below freezing.

When shrubs are used, the relationship between the plant and the container should be about equal. Large terra-cotta pots with a lip or without detailing are fine for shrubs. For plants like azaleas and geraniums with little significant height, a low container—a concrete pot, perhaps—is best, or use three-legged pots.

The following container plants for the small garden have been selected because they have some outstanding feature or because they grow with little care. The list is by no means complete, but rather a sampling of many fine plants for container growing.

SHRUBS FOR CONTAINER GARDENING

BOTANICAL AND COMMON NAME	MINIMUM NIGHT TEMPERATURE	GENERAL DESCRIPTION	REMARKS
Abutilon (flowering maple)	Tender	Bell-shaped flowers of paper-thin texture	Give plenty of water and sun
Azalea (see Rhododendron)	Check with nursery	Brilliant flowers, lush growth, many varieties	Great for portable gardens
Camellia japonica	5° to 10°F.	Handsome flowers in many colors	Excellent container plant
Camellia sasanqua	5° to 10°F.	Mostly small white flowers	Many varieties
Cotoneaster (many varieties)	Check with nursery	Glossy leaves, colorful berries	Small and large ones, many varieties
Fatsia japonica (aralia)	Tender	Foliage plant, fanlike leaves on tall stems	Makes bold appearance
Gardenia jasminoides	10° to 30°F.	Dark green leaves, fragrant white blooms	New varieties available
Hibiscus rosa-sinensis (Chinese hibiscus)	20° to 30°F.	Dark glossy green foliage, large flowers	Good performer in tubs or boxes
Ilex crenata (holly)	−5° to 5°F.	Glossy leaves, bright berries	Many good varieties
Juniperus communis depressa (prostrate juniper)	−50° to 35°F.	Blue green foliage	Forms dense mass
Juniperus chinensis 'Pfitzeriana' (pfitzer juniper)	−20° to −10°F.	Blue green foliage	Good screen plant
Ixora	Tender	Small red to white flowers	Splendid color in white tubs
Nerium oleander (oleander)	10° to 20°F.	Dark green leaves, bright flowers	Needs large container and lots of water
Osmanthus ilicifolius (holly olive)	−5° to 5°F.	Glossy leaves on upright stems	Grows fast in tubs

BOTANICAL AND COMMON NAME	MINIMUM NIGHT TEMPERATURE	GENERAL DESCRIPTION	REMARKS
✓ Pittosporum tobira	10° to 20°F.	Arching branches	Can be trained to shape
✓ Plumbago capensis (blue phlox)	20° to 30°F.	Small leaves, blue flowers	Robust grower
Podocarpus macrophyllus	Tender	Bright green leaves	Attractive in tubs
✓ Rhododendron (many)	Check with nursery	Many varieties	Excellent container plants
✓ Rose (many)	Check with nursery	All kinds and colors	Does very well in containers
Thuja occidentalis (arvorvitae)	−50° to −35°F.	Evergreens	Tough plants for untoward conditions
Viburnum (many)	Check with nursery	Attractive leaves, pretty flowers and berries	Many varieties
Yucca filamentosa (Spanish bayonet)	−20° to −10°F.	Blue green, sword-shaped leaves	Dramatic in tubs

TREES FOR CONTAINER GARDENING

BOTANICAL AND COMMON NAME	MINIMUM NIGHT TEMPERATURE	GENERAL DESCRIPTION	REMARKS
Acer palmatum (Japanese maple)	−10° to 0°F.	Lovely lacy leaves	Handsome in soy tub or round container
Araucaria excelsa (Norfolk pine)	Tender	Pyramid shape	Good vertical accent in Spanish flare-lip pot
Betula populifolia (gray birch)	−30° to −10°F.	Deciduous, irregular in shape	Fine tree for patio or along house wall
Cedrus atlantica glauca (blue atlas cedar)	0° to 10°F.	Needle evergreen with sprawling habit	Fine accent in large tubs near house corners
✓ Citrus (orange, lemon, lime)	Tender	Dark green leaves, nice branching effect	Excellent trees, indoors or out

BOTANICAL AND COMMON NAME	MINIMUM NIGHT TEMPERATURE	GENERAL DESCRIPTION	REMARKS
Eriobotrya japonica (loquat)	20° to 30°F.	Round headed with dark green leaves	Good for tubs and boxes
Ficus benjamina (weeping fig)	Tender	Tiny dark green leaves, branching habit	Good special effect in garden or indoors in tubs
✓ *Gingko biloba* (gingko)	−30° to −20°F.	Deciduous, lovely foliage	Handsome in containers, nice accent near house walls
✓ *Laburnum watereri* (goldenchain tree)	−20° to −10°F.	Deciduous, columnar shape	Good patio tub plant
✓ *Lagerstroemia indica* (crape myrtle)	−20° to −10°F.	Deciduous with pink flowers	Showy for patio
✓ *Magnolia soulangeana* (saucer magnolia)	−20° to −10°F.	Deciduous with round form, lovely flowers	Good near fence or wall
Malus sargentii (sargent crabapple)	−30° to −20°F.	Dwarf, round topped form	Perimeter decoration for paved area
Phellodendron amurense (cork tree)	−40° to −30°F.	Deciduous, attractive branching tree	For a special place
Phoenix loureirii (date palm)	Tender	Lovely, arching fronds	An indoor-outdoor favorite
✓ *Pinus mugo mughus* (mugho pine)	−40° to −30°F.	Irregular outline, broad and sprawling	To decorate paths, walks, and patios
Pinus parviflora glauca (Japanese white pine)	−10° to 0°F.	Needle evergreen with horizontal growth	Nice feature in and around garden
Pinus thunbergii (Japanese black pine)	−20° to −10°F.	Good spreading habit	Excellent container plant
Podocarpus gracilior	Tender	Graceful willowy branches	Good doorway plant
Rhapis excelsa (lady palm)	Tender	Dark green fan-shaped leaves	A stellar container plant

BOTANICAL AND COMMON NAME	MINIMUM NIGHT TEMPERATURE	GENERAL DESCRIPTION	REMARKS
Salix matsudana 'Tortuosa' (contorted Hankow willow)	−20° to −10°F.	Lovely sweeping branches	For a special place
Schefflera actinophylla (Australian umbrella tree)	Tender	Graceful stems tipped with fronds of leaves	Handsome in terra-cotta Spanish pot

9. The Small City Garden 🌿

A city garden is a haven for its owners, and now, with crowded city conditions, these pleasant retreats are needed more than ever. Small areas can be charming with some garden "props"—trellises, planters, canopies, and well-selected plants.

With most city gardens you will re-landscape rather than start fresh, so build around the existing trees and shrubs. Or if you decide on a new plan, select trees and shrubs with care. Either way, the city garden—even of postage-stamp size—is worth its space in gold.

Backyard Gardens

Some gardens will be a brick or slate patio; others will be merely a path with flower beds. Consider what kind of outdoor area you want before you start. Observe the sunniest areas and reserve them for flowers. Decide on the personality of the area; will it be formal, Italian, Japanese, rustic, or modern California style? Try to follow one dominant theme; it's easier to work with than a combination of ideas. And always, of course, be sure the theme is in keeping with the architecture of the house.

To integrate the garden and the house, planting beds and paved areas are needed. Although the rectangular shape is the easiest to to cope with, it often lacks the charm and grace that is found in gentle curves of free-form lines.

You will need fences and walls in your garden for privacy and decoration. And even though most retreats will already have some kind of barrier, fences are bound to need repair. Thus, always start fresh because new materials (plastic, perforated concrete) have given

us new kinds of barriers. If you have a small shady area, select a
fretwork fence so that light can enter. Vines on the fence look good
and ensure privacy.

This city garden is expertly designed with planter boxes of flowers, a wall of leafy green on the left. On the right are contained plantings, naturally grown. Photo by Molly Adams.

Be wary of very tall (over six feet) fences because they look formidable and may be out of scale in the city gardens. And do consult your neighbors about a fence; they may even share part of the cost. In most cases a five- or six-foot fence is adequate.

An overhead structure like a canopy or trellis is possible for backyard gardens, but it usually is not necessary unless there are overhead neighbors. Even then, a tree does the job just as well.

Paths and paved areas are vital in the small garden; consider them first before you do any planting. Because of the limited space, keep paths to a minimum. Paving stones or cross sections of tree trunks called "rounds" are pleasing because they create design whereas a straight path tends to be monotonous. Borders for paths and flower beds (brick or concrete stone) are other accents that add attractiveness to the design.

99

If soil is bad in the city garden, put in raised beds for plantings. This adds depth to the soil, and beds put plants at a height where they can be better seen by visitors. Raised beds can be dry walls of fieldstone, mortar walls of concrete, or brick or redwood planters. All are do-it-yourself weekend projects.

In city gardens there is no natural background landscape of trees and shrubs; the visitor sees only the confines of the garden, so what you grow is quite important. All plants should be healthy, lovely, and complemented by some garden feature—a bench, a piece of statuary in a strategic place, or a fountain or tiny pool. Generally, these items are best situated in the rear of the garden near a fence or in a corner where they stand out. Choose the prop carefully, so that it will blend with the overall effect of the yard. Make this the focal point of the garden and put it in the perfect place.

In the city, seasonal container plants are stellar attractions. Group pots of geraniums or chrysanthemums for a real splash of color at patio corners, in rows, along paths, or near fences. Use annuals in low redwood boxes, pots of spring bulbs for instant color, and evergreens for winter accent.

Plants for Backyard Gardens

Azalea	Japanese holly
Flowering quince	Japanese maple
White dogwood	Dwarf boxwood
Mountain laurel	Firethorn
Rock cotoneaster	Climbing roses
Hemlock	Boston ivy

DOORWAY GARDENS

A doorway garden is a small piece of hospitality. Don't leave this area barren; the well-considered use of a few plants can make these tiny areas welcome spots. Simply decorated twin ceramic tubs filled with foliage plants like ivy or fatshedera are perfect to grace a simple white door of a Colonial home, but be wary of the plant's scale. Height and mass should be in good balance to the size of the door. (In winter the tubbed plants can be moved indoors.) If there are steps leading to the doorway, use twin tubs of foliage plants that have mass and volume, but be sure they do not impede traffic.

A formal entrance porch with a roof needs some low and round box hedges in front of it and perhaps a pair of large white boxes filled with small ginkgoes.

Antique urns filled with flowering plants set on brick platforms (two feet high and two feet square) add grace and charm to any doorway. If your entrance is severely plain, consider the use of a long redwood plant box filled with foliage plants; this arrangement smooths the transition from outdoors to indoors.

Sometimes even a single specimen plant like a tall podocarpus in a handsome jardiniere by the side of the door is all that is needed to create the welcome look. For an L-shaped doorway, consider planters filled with vines like clematis or bougainvillea; this is indeed a colorful display in the summer.

Set away from the crowded city, a tiny terrace is a pleasant retreat for the home-owner. G. Woodard photo.

THE TINY TERRACE

There are hidden, out-of-the-way little spaces that can become attractive greeneries rather than bare areas. They are much like a doorway garden and need careful planning to make them effective.

Because of the very limited space, use small trees in corners and try to work in a terrace box. (If possible, try to include one small container tree like a Japanese maple for accent.) Adorn walls with brackets for plants and use hanging baskets wherever possible. Window boxes work well in these areas if there is a railing or a parapet.

102

In the city container plants are worth their weight in gold; this is a charming container garden. Photo by Roger Scharmer.

Nestled between buildings, this small appealing terrace is a relaxing place to escape to. Photo by Roger Scharmer.

PLANT MATERIALS THAT MAY BE GROWN UNDER CITY CONDITIONS

Deciduous Trees

Betula alba (white birch)
Carpinus betulus (European hornbeam)
Cornus florida (flowering dogwood)
Crataegus cordata (Washington thorn)
C. oxyacantha (English hawthorn)
Ginkgo biloba (Ginkgo)

Ilex opaca (American holly)
Magnolia glauca (swamp magnolia)
M. soulangeana (saucer magnolia)
M. stellata (star magnolia)
Malus—species and varieties (flowering crabs)
Prunus subhirtella (Japanese flowering cherry)
Sophora japonica (Chinese scholar tree)
Styrax japonica (snowbell tree)
Syringa pekinensis (Pekin lilac)
Ulmus pumila (dwarf Asiatic elm)

Evergreen Trees

Pinus mugo (Mugo pine)
P. sylvestris (Scots pine)
Taxus cuspidata (Japanese yew)
Thuyu occidentalis (arborvitae)

Deciduous Shrubs

Acanthopanax pentaphyllum (fiveleaf aralia)
Azaleas (many species)
Berberis thunbergii (Japanese barberry)
Deutzia scabra (rough deutzia)
Forsythia (all species)
Hibiscus syriacus (rose-of-Sharon)
Lagerstroemia indica (crape-myrtle)
Ligustrum ibota (ibota privet)
L. ovalifolium (California privet)
Myrica carolinensis (bayberry)
Nandina domestica (heavenly bamboo)
Philadelphus (mock orange)
Rhus cotinus (smokebush)
Spiraea Vanhouttei (Vanhoutte's spirea)
Symphoricarpos vulgaris (snowberry)
Syringa vulgaris (lilac)
Vitex agnus-castus (chaste tree)
Weigela (hybrids; weigela)

Evergreen Shrubs

Buxus microphylla Koreana (Korean box)
Ilex crenata (all varieties; Japanese holly)
Kalmia latifolia (mountain laurel)
Osmanthus aquifolium (holly olive)
Pieris japonica (andromeda)
Pyracantha coccinea (firethorn)
Rhododendron carolinianum
R. hybrids
R. mucronulatum

Vines

Cobaea scandens (cup and saucer vine)
Hedera helix (English ivy)
Parthenocissus tricuspidata (Boston ivy)
P. quinquefolia (Virginia creeper)
Phaseolus coccineus (scarlet runner bean)
Polgonum aubertii (Chinese fleece vine)
Wisteria floribunda (Japanese wisteria)

10. Special Gardens for Small Areas ✒

Even in the small garden it is possible to have a special section of herbs, vegetables, or even roses. Indeed, the herb and vegetable garden can be grown in a five- by ten-foot area and provide enough seasonings and greens for the average family all summer. A rose garden, too, can—with clever design—be done on a diminutive scale.

Plan these gardens carefully; use every inch of available space. Although they may not be as grandiose as their larger counterparts, they offer great satisfaction to the homeowner.

HERB GARDENS

Herb gardens were once patterned upon somewhat intricate lines. Today's herb garden is much less formal. It generally is a simple one and can be put in place in a weekend. Some plan is necessary, but elaborate designs are not needed. Yet for all its simplicity, the herb garden can be a delightful scene of foliage textures and colors joining with flower form and gentle color.

The small herb garden close to the kitchen is, of course, a convenience. Or the garden can be used as an accent away from the house; here, of course, a more formal design might be needed. But no matter where you put the garden, choose a sunny place, because herbs do not do well in shaded areas. The garden should be neat and weeded, with paths and some borders to set it off in the landscape. A good background, such as a wall or fence or even a hedge, helps too.

The garden design can take many shapes—wagonwheel, butterfly, knot—and the garden can have herbs for fragrance, flavor, and medicinal uses. Herbs are divided into several groups, although there is some overlapping. Those grown for fragrance are known as aromatic herbs, culinary herbs are used for cooking seasonings, and medicinal herbs have an infinite variety of uses. There is special charm in a herb garden, and it is a delight to be able to pick your own seasonings.

Select a well-drained site for the herb garden; a place with a slight slope is good, so that water will not stand around plant crowns. Most herbs prefer a neutral or slightly alkaline soil, so, if your soil is acid, apply liberal amounts of limestone to the garden each spring. Be sure the site has plenty of sun; eight hours daily is ideal, but most herbs will (if necessary) tolerate only four hours.

To prepare the garden, stake out the area with string and stakes. Remove any debris, large stones, and weeds. Work the soil until it is porous and crumbly. Dig down at least twelve inches (eighteen inches would be better), and prepare the ground carefully so the plants will thrive. Do not attempt to plant in dry clay soils, or the herbs will die.

Hardy perennial herbs are bought as young plants, and annuals and biennials are started yearly from seed. Put perennials in the ground in spring, and, when frost danger is over, sow seed for the annuals and biennials. Sprinkle the seeds over prepared soil and then cover with a light layer of soil. Moisten thoroughly with a fine mist.

Germination of seed varies with the herb, so don't panic if some herbs take a long time to sprout. Keep the plants reasonably moist during this time. Most seeds should be planted in the spring, but herbs such as thyme, dill, and parsley can be sown in summer too. Herbs should be cut just as the flowers are about to open and when the essential oils are most abundant.

Herb gardens are ornamental as well as useful; over two dozen herbs grow in this plot. Photo by Roche.

Herbs for Fragrance

✓ Basil *(Ocimum minimum)*

✓ Bergamot *(Monarda didyma)*

Geranium (Pelargonium)

    Pelargonium crispum (citronella geranium)

    P. denticulatum (skeleton geranium)

    P. graveolens (rose geranium)

  ✓ *P. limoneum* (lemon geranium)

    P. melissinum (balm geranium)

    P. odoratissimum (in variety)

✓ Lavender *(Lavandula)*

    Lavandula dentata

    L. spica

    L. vera

Lavender-cotton *(Santolina chamaecyparissus)*

✓ Marjoram *(Origanum)*

✓ Mint *(Mentha)*

    Mentha citrata (orange mint)

    M. crispa (curled mint)

  ✓ *M. rotundifolia* (apple mint)

✓ Rosemary *(Rosmarinus officinalis)*

✓ Rue *(Ruta graveolens)*

✓ Savory *(Satureja)*

    Satureja hortensis (summer savory)

    S. montana (winter savory)

✓ Southernwood *(Artemisia abrotanum)*

✓ Thyme *(Thymus)* in varieties

✓ Verbena, lemon *(Lippia citriodora)*

✓ Woodruff, sweet *(Asperula odorata)*

HERB CHART

COMMON AND BOTANICAL NAME	ANNUAL, BIENNIAL, PERENNIAL	COMMON AND BOTANICAL NAME	ANNUAL, BIENNIAL, PERENNIAL
Anise *(Pimpinella anisum)*	A	Lovage *(Levisticum officinale)*	P
Balm (lemon balm) *(Melissa officinalis)*	P	Mint, apple *(Mentha rotundifolia)*	P
Basil *(Ocimum minimum)*	A	Mint, curled *(Mentha crispa)*	P
Bergamot *(Monarda fistulosa)*	P	Parsley *(Petroselinum hortense)*	B
Borage *(Borago officinalis)*	A	Peppermint *(Mentha piperita)*	P
Chamomile *(Anthemis nobilis, Matricaria chamomilla)*	P	Rosemary *(Rosmarinus officinalis)*	P
Chervil *(Anthriscus cerefolium)*	A	Rue *(Ruta graveolens)*	P
Chives *(Allium schoenoprasum)*	P	Saffron *(Crocus sativus)*	P
Coriander *(Coriandrum sativum)*	A	Sage *(Salvia officinalis)*	P
Cumin *(Cuminum cyminum)*	A	Savory, summer *(Satureja hortensis)*	A
Dill *(Anethum graveolens)*	A	Savory, winter *(Satureja montana)*	P
Fennel flower *(Nigella sativa)*	A	Sorrel *(Rumex acetosa)*	P
Geranium, scented in variety *(Pelargonium)*	P	Southernwood *(Artemisia abrotanum)*	P
Horseradish *(Armoracia rusticana)*	P	Spearmint *(Mentha spicata)*	P
Lavender *(Lavandula vera, officinalis, spica, dentata)*	P	Sweet basil *(Ocimum basilicum)*	A
Lavender-cotton *(Santolina chamaecyparissus)*	P	Sweet fennel *(Foeniculum officinale)*	A
Lemon verbena *(Lippia citriodora)*	P	Sweet flag *(Acorus calamus)*	P
		Sweet marjoram *(Origanum majorana)*	A

COMMON AND BOTANICAL NAME	ANNUAL, BIENNIAL, PERENNIAL	COMMON AND BOTANICAL NAME	ANNUAL, BIENNIAL, PERENNIAL
Sweet woodruff (*Asperula odorata*)	P	Thyme (*Thymus*)	P
Tansy (*Tanacetum vulgare*)	P	Watercress (*Nasturtium-aquaticum*)	P
Tarragon (*Artemisia dracunculus*)	P		

ROSE GARDENS

Roses are popular flowers with a romance of their own. They have been with us for a very long time and continue to be admired and grown. A well-designed rose garden is indeed a stunning sight.

In planning this garden choose a place that has some air circulation, but is still protected from the wind. Try to select a neutral background, so that the roses will be seen to their best advantage. Install brick or fieldstone paths to enhance the beauty of the garden, and decide upon a definite pattern for the beds.

Roses need a fertile, well-drained, slightly acid soil with a pH ranging from 5.5 to 6.5. Because rose roots are long, dig deeply, to about twenty inches. Take out an additional three to six inches, and replace with cinders or crushed stone to ensure good drainage facilities. Roses will grow in a fairly clayey or sandy soil, but they will not thrive unless drainage is almost perfect and the soil is fertile.

For good rose bloom, be sure the garden is in a sunny spot; roses need about five hours of sun daily. Some shade is beneficial in the afternoon.

In the first season of growth, feeding may not be necessary if the original planting was done with care. In the second year start a fertilization program; roses are heavy feeders and need nitrogen, phosphorus, and potash. Give them at least two or three feedings a year: the first in spring soon after pruning, the second in June before bloom, and the third in summer. I use a 5-10-5 fertilizer for roses, but check in your area to see what is being used with most success. Be sure the soil is moist when applying fertilizer and work it into the soil around plants with a rake.

Roses may be planted in the autumn or in the early spring. Be sure the crown of the plant is one to two inches below the soil surface. Pack soil firmly around the roots; avoid loose planting.

Pruning depends upon the type of rose and the locality, but there are some general rules to remember. Remove dead or weak wood and maintain the desired height. Use sharp pruning shears and make a slant cut above a vigorous bud. To guard against fungi, treat the ends of cut stems with a fungicide.

Roses need an evenly moist soil throughout the growing season, and do give them deep soakings rather than frequent light sprinklings. Don't give them overhead watering, since it can cause black spots to form on the foliage.

Handsome roses frame this terrace, a perfect setting for the small garden. Photo by Roche.

The amount of winter protection depends on the weather in your locality and the type of rose; check in your area for this information.

PLANTING AND CARE

Planting distances depend upon the type of rose. For hybrid and tea roses a distance of eighteen to twenty-four inches apart is fine. Floribundas and grandifloras need more space—about eighteen to thirty-six inches between each plant. Trim the roses before you plant them, and remove broken or injured roots. As mentioned, plant roses deep and place them in position, so that the crown (point of union between the stock and scion) is between one to two inches below the surface of the soil. In mild climates the bud union should be just

114

above the surface of the soil. After planting, pack the soil firmly around the roots and keep the roses well watered the first few weeks until they are established.

Roses need pruning to produce strong roots and shoots; without proper cutting they get leggy and dense. In spring before growth starts, prune plants just above a node (bud); cut in a slanting direction and leave three to five buds on each stem. Only light pruning is needed for rambler roses that bloom on old wood. The ramblers that bloom on new wood from the base of the plant need pruning after flowering.

The planting time depends upon your climate. In cold areas, early spring is best for setting out dormant bushes. In the midpart of the country, early spring or late fall is suggested, and in all-year climates, roses can be planted from November to January.

Bare-root plants are most often selected by gardeners. These are dormant and ready to start a new cycle of growth when you get them.

The garden of this small property is devoted to roses. Photo courtesy of Star Roses.

If you cannot plant them immediately, keep them cool and be sure the roots are kept moist. Never allow rose roots to become dry before they are planted. Put them in water until you get the plants in the ground. Packaged roses are often seen, and, if they have been stored in a cool place, they are satisfactory. If the branches look dry and shriveled, chances are they have been kept in a hot location, so don't buy them. Container-grown roses are already started for you and cost more than dormant ones, but for beginners these are the best buy.

In cold regions, plants should be protected for the winter. Place mounds of soil about ten inches high around them. Do not scoop the soil from around the plant; rather, bring in fresh soil. Remove the covering gradually in spring when growth starts.

Because there are so many roses available, first decide what kind you want. The following partial list should help you:

Good for display and cutting, garden roses include hybrid teas, floribundas, and grandifloras. The hybrid teas have a sturdy growing habit and are hardy in the north if given suitable winter protection. They give generous bloom from June to September. Some varieties grow over three feet, others are low growers. There is a wide range of color and form.

Floribunda varieties vary greatly in size; some are almost dwarf and others grow to six feet. Flower form is single to semidouble in a wide range of colors. These plants are very floriferous and less demanding than most roses.

Grandifloras are very vigorous, free-blooming, and easy to grow. The flowers are born in clusters and last very well.

Edging roses are dwarf, generally of the *polyantha* group. They are very hardy and give generous bloom throughout the season.

Hedge roses are quick growing, tall and bushy, and they require very little care.

Old-fashioned roses generally have single flowers and include old favorites, such as provence rose and the damask rose.

Climbing roses can be trained to supports; some are rampant, but others are more restrained in growth, and some have a peak season of bloom while others flower intermittently throughout the season. A few varieties are very hardy, but others are suitable only for mild climates.

11. Modular Gardens for Problem Areas ✑

Similar to container gardening (and perhaps it can be included in that term), modular gardening is growing plants in boxes and arranging the boxes in appealing geometric groups. The boxes—squares, rectangles, parallelograms—are placed side by side to carry out endless patterns. For small areas this is a highly effective way to use plants. In handsome boxes they seem more than they really are and appear dramatic; the size of the garden is forgotten in the beauty of the patterns created with boxes. Further, this portable gardening provides color and accent where and when you want it in the landscape. It is easy gardening; no weeding, mulching, or exacting care is needed.

The garden can be on a deck, patio, or any place within the property. Besides its visual appeal, the modular garden gives the homeowner a chance to have a garden even if the soil on his property will not support plants.

The somewhat formal geometric patterns created by the planter boxes are best suited to the contemporary house or to formal architecture. For the rustic or cottage home, the familiar garden in standard pots and tubs is more suitable.

Modular gardens depend on the right combination of different-sized boxes in assorted patterns. Vary the heights and the widths; have tall and short ones. Butt them together or line them against a fence; use them in an L-shaped pattern or in a herringbone design. Remember that you are concerned with a *combination* of boxes for this is the modular concept of design. If one arrangement is not pleasing, move the boxes until you find the right treatment for the area. The overall pattern created by the boxes is the garden.

THE BOXES

Flats are wooden boxes that nurseries use to grow seedlings; they consist of four sides and two boards across the bottom. Modular boxes are similarly designed. You have to build boxes at home (commercial planters are not available), but it is an easy project. The dimensions will vary for each box, so draw the entire plan on paper before you start the actual construction.

Redwood is the best material; as mentioned, it needs no preservatives and will last for years. Douglas fir is stronger than redwood, but more costly. It is best for large boxes (over sixteen inches square), and it needs a protective coating. Glue and screw all corners of wood containers or nail them together securely. Use one-inch stock for most boxes, two-inch boards for large ones.

You can build all kinds of boxes: small (three inches deep for small bulbs and annuals), medium (for shrubs), and large (twenty-four inches long for trees). Thus, what goes into the box will determine how deep it should be.

PLANTING THE BOXES

Almost any plant can be grown in a box temporarily; some plants such as camellias and azaleas do better in containers where roots are confined, and the size of the plant does not become cumbersome. It is possible to cater to the plants' needs with the right soil and light. Prepare the boxes carefully; it is about all you will have to do to start the garden.

Be sure that the bottom boards are placed one-fourth-inch apart, so that excess water can drain freely. Put in a two-inch bed of small stones or chipped gravel (for twelve- by sixteen-inch box), scatter a few lumps of charcoal over the bed, and fill with a good garden soil of equal parts humus and loam. Water the plants thoroughly after planting, and attend to them the first few weeks until they become established. Then they can grow on their own with adequate moisture.

This deck is being readied for modular gardens. The boxes will be set into appropriate niches. The geometrical form is pleasing and, once plants are in place, the area becomes a maintenance-free garden. Photo courtesy of California Redwood Association.

Boxes for modular gardens can be set in infinite patterns, and all kinds of plants can be used in them. Photo courtesy of California Redwood Association; Douglas Baylis, landscape architect.

Plant the box where it is going to be in the landscape plan; container pots and tubs can be moved on dollies but modular gardens are permanent once installed.

ANNUALS

Most commonly grown annuals, available at nurseries, are ideal for modular gardens because their roots are shallow. Container annuals add immediate color to a terrace or garden, and with proper care they bloom for a long time. Low-growing annuals like petunias give stellar splashes of concentrated color. Tall ones like *Celosia plumosa* are excellent for vertical accent against a terrace wall or a fence. Several boxes of rain lilies (Schizanthus) are charming on the patio or terrace.

120

Several different annuals in a redwood box (for example, a bouquet of balsam in the center surrounded by vivid blue lobelia) are stunning, and for fragrance nicotiana placed in tapered bowls makes an unbeatable display. Annuals provide a constant flow of color all summer.

Use a good general potting mix and feed plants biweekly. Water them heavily on warm days and be sure that they get some sunshine.

Browallia speciosa. Amethyst flower with small, violet, white-throated flowers. Needs bright light and copious water. Blooms through spring and summer.

Cineraria. Lovely blue, purple, red, crimson, and white flowers. Blooms freely in partial shade and coolness. Looks best in low, standard clay pots.

Impatiens. Many varieties with double flowers in pink, white, or lavender. Give plants sunlight and feeding. Handsome in tubs or boxes.

Lobelia. Vivid blue, also a pale blue variety. Summer through fall color. Excellent small plants.

Petunias (all kinds). Easy to grow. Blooms for months in a wide color range—white, purple, pink, lavender, red, and a new yellow. Dwarf, trailing, and large ruffled varieties available. Give them sunlight and water. For a really stunning effect, grow a mass of one variety in a large cube redwood container.

Primrose. Many species and varieties in pink, lavender, or white. Nice for window boxes and border decoration. Likes some shade.

PERENNIALS

Perennials provide continuous summer color. Geraniums, tuberous begonias, and chrysanthemums are only a few of the many plants at seasonal time.

All perennials must have a rest period sometime during the year. Those that bloom in summer rest over the winter; the winter plants rest in summer. (The season of bloom depends on your individual climate.)

Acanthus mollis (Grecian urn plant). Large, with rosettes of dark green leaves and erect spikes of white and lilac flowers in green bracts. Blooms easily with little care. Needs large tub.

Campanula isophylla (bellflower). Blue star-shaped flowers. Needs plenty of water and partial shade. A small plant that requires an ornate container.

Chrysanthemum. Excellent for autumn because of its many sizes and colors. Many flower as late as November. Pinch back plants in early part of season, and be sure that soil is always moderately wet. Sunshine is best, although some varieties bloom in partial shade. Chrysanthemums are well suited to low, standard clay pots or white shallow bowls.

Geranium. 'Lady Washington' varieties. Dark green, heart-shaped leaves. Pink, red, lavender, or white flowers with and without markings. Garden geranium is *Pelargonium hortorum*. Round leaves with scalloped margins, often with color zone in center. Single or double flowers in shades of white, pink, red, or salmon. Groups of potted geraniums around posts, at entrance door, or at terrace corners are handsome. A very large low tub filled with many geraniums is equally attractive.

Helleborus. Several species: Christmas-rose, *H. niger*; Lenten rose, *H. orientalis*. Both good for boxes and tubs.

Hosta (plantain lily). Big, with lush green leaves. A very decorative plant for difficult areas because it often blooms in dense shade. Easy to grow; best in squatty tubs.

Lantana. Robust, hard-to-kill plants that bear many flowers month after month. Give them full sunlight and rather dry soil. Trailing lantana (*L. montevidensis*) with purple flowers is especially nice for hanging baskets.

Tuberous begonia. Spectacular flowers in a wide range of colors. Single and double, ruffled, camellia, and rose forms. Needs coolness; difficult to grow in heat. Excellent for hanging redwood baskets.

BULBS

Potted bulbs offer early spring color, a succession of bloom through many months, and are lovely in the modular garden.

Many spring bulbs can be planted in the late fall and stored over the winter in a cool, dark, shaded spot—a basement or pantry—and brought into the house in early winter. Leaves will be pale yellow and white from a lack of light, but foliage turns green and growth starts in a matter of days with bright sunlight. When it is safely warm outside, move bulbs to the terrace or patio.

A modular garden is being started on this deck; square and rectangular shapes in pleasing patterns are the essence of this kind of gardening. Photo courtesy of California Redwood Association.

After they flower take the bulbs inside, but don't cut off the foliage. Keep it growing until the leaves begin to yellow, and then gradually let the soil dry. When the foliage and soil are dry, take the bulbs from the container and store them in brown paper sacks in a cool place for fall planting.

A good soil mix for bulbs is three parts garden loam, one part sand, and one part leaf mold. For a concentration of color, plant bulbs close together. To start bulbs, cover the bottom of the container with pebbles. Fill the pot about one-third full of soil, and set the bulbs on top. Till in and around until the tips are barely covered.

Achimenes. Pretty color from charming small plants. Plants come in a variety of colors. All need sunlight and plenty of water.

Autumn crocus. Dramatic tulip-shaped flowers in a brilliant yellow, lavender, or rose color. Several planted in a redwood box or shallow clay pot make a showy display in August and September. Grow them quite wet in partial shade. For contrast, set crocus in pots on brick floors or against paved walls.

Daffodil. Many varieties bloom from January to May. Most of the easy-to-grow ones sparkle with color in planters and window boxes. Plant bulbs in late fall. When growth starts, move them to sunshine and keep them liberally watered.

Hyacinth. Much color for little effort. A hardy bulb with bright green leaves and fragrant flowers in white, pink, or blue. Needs lots of sunlight and water. Blooms in March and April.

Kaffir lily. Nurseries stock mature plants in pots for spring bloom. Very dramatic with clusters of vivid orange or red flowers, the Kaffir lily deserves a spot on the terrace. Looks grand in large, round tubs and can be grown in the same container for several years.

Shrubs and Trees for Modular and Deck Gardens

Acer circinatum (vine maple)—lovely color in autumn

Aeonium arboreum—ornamental leaf rosettes; grows well in shallow containers

Agave attenuata—will thrive for many years in large tub

Aloe arborescens—spiny leaves; beautiful winter blooms

Araucaria heterophylla—dark green horizontal branches in symmetrical designs

Aucuba japonica—shiny dark green leaves, ovate or oblong; decorative doorway plant

Azalea, Kurume—dense, striking foliage; blooms profusely

Bambusa (bamboo)—woody grasses with variations in stem color

Buxus microphylla japonica (box)—trim into formal shapes; decorative plant for entries and balconies

B. sempervirens (common box)—shiny dark green leaves, dense foliage; striking when trimmed into formal shapes.

Camellia japonica—attractive foliage when not in bloom; wonderful container plant

C. sasanqua—shiny green leaves; blooms profusely in autumn.

Cedrus deodara (deodar cedar)—dark bluish green leaves; makes a lovely Christmas tree

Chaenomeles 'Contorta' (flowering quince)—twisted and contorted branches; early spring bloomer

Chamaedorea elegans—feathery leaves; plant in groups

Crataegus phaenopyrum (Washington thorn)—white flowers; red berries in winter; beautiful fall color

Dion edule—feathery leaves; thrives in sunshine

Elaeagnus pungens—trim to shape; likes a sunny location

Fagus sylvatica (European beech)—shiny dark green leaves that turn reddish brown in autumn

F. sylvatica 'Purpurea-pendula'—striking weeping beech; thrives for years in a large pot

Fatshedera lizei—shiny green leaves resembling giant ivy

Fatsia japonica 'Moseri'—glossy bold leaves; attractive plant in entries

Ficus benjamina (fig)—broad, with graceful branches; a good focal point for patio

Gardenia jasminoides (cape-jasmine)—thick leaves; needs warm atmosphere

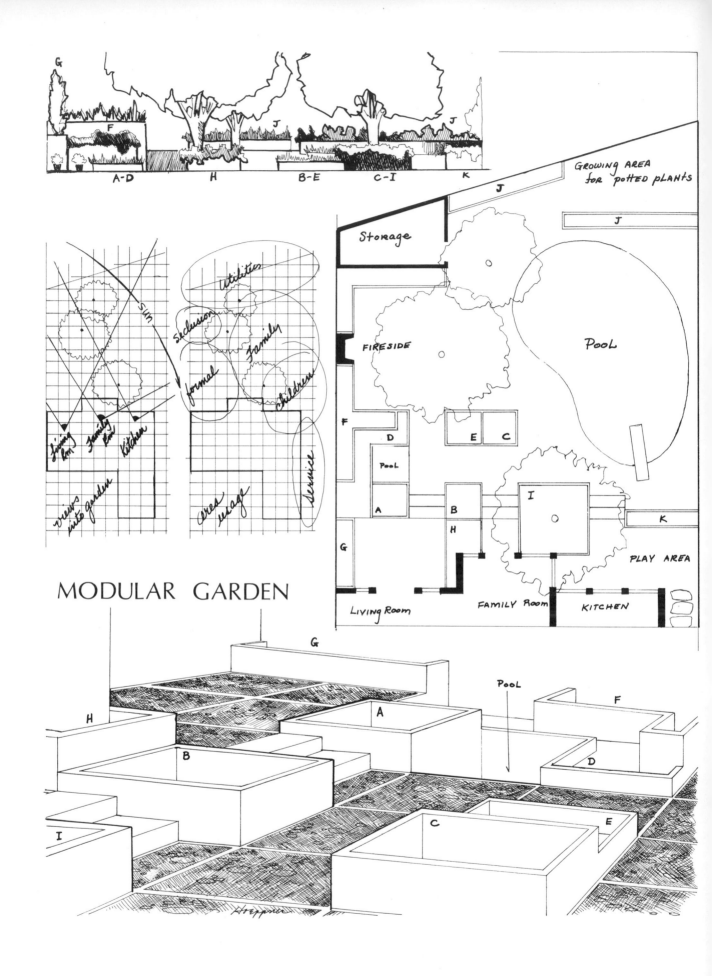

G F A-D H J B-E C-I J K

GROWING AREA for potted plants

Storage

FIRESIDE

POOL

J

F D E C

Pool

A B I K

G H

PLAY AREA

Living Room FAMILY Room KITCHEN

sun

Utilities
Seclusion
formal Family
children
Service

Living Rm Family Rm Kitchen

views into garden

areas usage

MODULAR GARDEN

G

H

POOL

F

A

B

D

I

C

E

Ginkgo biloba (maidenhair tree)—beautiful brilliant yellow leaves in the fall

Juniperus chinensis 'Torulosa' (juniper)—twisted, windblownlike branches; especially attractive in aggregate containers

Laurus nobilis (laurel)—dark and glossy green leaves; attractive when trimmed to form topiary shapes

Ligustrum lucidum (privet)—thick leathery leaves; small white flowers

Lily. Excellent patio plant, but its color does not last long enough for me. All kinds of lilies are available from summer to fall, depending upon the varieties.

Lime, Rangpur—dense foliage; provides fruit all year

Osmanthus fragrans—fragrant white flowers; attractive at entrance-ways

Phormuim tenax (New Zealand)—grows to considerable size; thrives even when neglected

Phyllostachys nigra (black-joint bamboo)—green and black stems; unsurpassed for an oriental motif

P. viridi-glaucescens—attractive yellow stems

Picea glauca 'Conica'—symmetrical appearance; excellent outdoors Christmas tree

Pieris japonica—drooping flower clusters that provide year-round beauty

Pinus thunbergii (Japanese black pine)—uneven, upright branches; a slow-growing tree

Pittosporum phillyaeoides (narrow-leaved pittosporum)—drooping branchlets; grows well in sunny location

P. undulatum (Victorian box)—fragrant blossoms; attractive when trained to form a small single-stemmed tree

Podocarpus gracilior—superb plant for entranceways

P. macrophylla maki—small leaves; shrubby

Prunus blirieana (cherry plum)—red purple foliage

P. serrulata—striking clustered flowers; blooms in spring

Rhapis excelsa—fanlike leaves; attractive when planted in clumps

Rhododendron 'Bric-a-Brac'—white blossoms in the winter; low-growing plant

Rosa (rose)—plant in large containers as roots should not be cramped

Tsuga canadensis 'Pendula'—weeping branches; slow growing

12. Basic Maintenance

Landscaping demands basic needs—composts, fertilizer, insect prevention, pruning, and tools and equipment. An understanding of these needs helps you to keep your property looking good; once you have invested time, labor, and money, it is senseless to have insects ruin the scheme or have plants die from lack of nutrients. Pruning trees and shrubs is necessary too as a matter of good grooming.

Vacuum cleaners and brooms are needed to clean a home; tools and equipment are necessary to keep the garden looking attractive. Usually a gardener neglects his grounds because he lacks implements, so keep tools on hand.

COMPOSTS

Good soil is necessary to grow any plant successfully and the stuff it is made of is compost. This is decomposing organic matter that you can stockpile on your grounds to improve soil. Preparing compost is working with nature; it involves leaves, lawn clippings, old plants, small twigs, and food scraps in a small pile. Have the compost heap in an inconspicuous but accessible place; the area does not have to be larger than five square feet. I use two- by four-feet boards on three sides to keep the compost heap in place and to help hide it.

Add manure and lime to the compost as you collect it. The wastes are turned into compost by bacteria, fungi, and other microscopic or minute organisms. Moisture is necessary to promote decomposition, but use reasonable amounts of water; the material should not be too wet or too dry. Allow air to permeate the vegetable wastes so that decomposition takes place. Occasionally poke holes into the compost with a rake handle. Try to keep the pile concave so that it will catch water and turn the compost now and then.

Put leaves, lawn trimmings, weeds, nonwoody prunings, annual and perennial remains, banana skins, and so forth in the pile. (Do *not* put evergreen leaves, pine shavings, or sawdust into it.) When the materials have decomposed, the compost will be black or dark brown. Decomposition time depends on climate, material used, and other variables.

MULCHES

Mulching is using peat moss, salt hay, leaves, or any available similar material—such as fir bark (potting medium for orchids) or a prepared mulch like Ko-Ko-O (dry outer shell of cocoa bean)—to give plants winter protection. Apply the mulch to the surface of the soil around the plants to prevent loss of soil moisture by evaporation and to keep weeds down. Use a mulch that is coarse enough to admit water, but not too much moisture.

When you use mulch, you are giving plants more than warmth; you are protecting them against alternating thawing and freezing, cold winds, and winter sunlight. Mulching also reduces the depth to which frost penetrates, and although it cannot totally prevent erosion, it helps somewhat. Mulch can be from two to five inches deep, but do not apply it until the top few inches of the soil are frozen.

FERTILIZATION

After a while plants deplete soil of nutrients, so feeding is necessary. Do not confuse fertilizers with soil conditioners that help to keep soil porous and crumbly. Plants obtain many elements from the soil, but the three most important are nitrogen, phosphorus, and potassium. Nitrogen produces good leaf and stem growth with rich green color, phosphorus promotes root development and helps to ripen tissues, and potassium gives plants vigor and helps them to ward off diseases.

There are inorganic fertilizers—minerals and synthetic minerals—and organic fertilizers—manure, bone meal, dried blood, peat, etc. It is necessary to use a combination of both types to maintain and balance the sources of plant nutrition.

Complete fertilizers provide nitrogen, phosphorus, and potassium in varying proportions. A 5-10-5 fertilizer has five pounds available nitrogen, ten pounds phosphoric acid, and five pounds potash to each one hundred pounds.

There are dozens of fertilizers. Some are for lawns; others are for evergreens, roses, and so forth. The labels on the package tell you how much to use per square foot, and it is best not to overdo it. After feeding, water the plants so that nutrients penetrate the soil. Wash leaves and stems so that they will not get burned by the chemicals. Spread fertilizers evenly and thinly; don't pile them in a heap. Feed trees and shrubs by sprinkling fertilizer on the ground or by boring holes in the soil to about eighteen inches and filling with fertilizers.

Pests and Diseases

You will never win the war against pests and blight, but you can keep trouble to a minimum by being observant and by using safe controls (including natural predators such as birds and insects) when necessary. Inspect stems and leaves frequently to be sure that pests aren't getting a foothold, for once entrenched, they are tough to get rid of. While massing for an attack, however, they can be eradicated without resorting to strong poisons.

Persistent chlorinated hydrocarbon insecticides are harmful to the world ecosystem, for they remain in the chain of nature and should not be used. These include products that contain Aldrin, Chlordane, DDT, Dieldrin, Endrin, Heptachlor, Kelthane, Lindane, Methoxychlor, Tedion, and Toxaphene (not a complete list). Botanical repellents made from plants, such as pyrethrum and rotenone, are generally preferable to the synthetic poisons in fighting insects. If necessary, some of the synthetics, such as Malathion and Sevin, might have to be used in the battle of the bugs, but they are still poisons and should be handled with great respect. Of course, nonpoisonous controls—dormant oils, plain water, and natural predators, such as birds, lacewings, ladybugs, and praying mantises—are the best controls. Insects are now available from insectaries, listed in gardeners' magazines.

Most insects that attack gardens can be seen and for the most part are easily subdued. Some pests, of course, are microscopic, but the damage they do can readily be seen in leaves and stems.

Fungi and bacteria that produce plant disease also produce symp-

Ladybugs are the gardener's friend; they eat a multitude of insects—especially aphids, a common garden pest. Photos courtesy of United States Department of Agriculture.

Birds, too, have their place in a garden, for they consume many kinds of garden insects. Photo courtesy of United States Department of Agriculture.

toms—visible clues in the appearance of the plant. Keep a watchful eye for signs of trouble in the garden and catch it before it starts.

Chewing insects, like cutworms, caterpillars, some beetles, and leaf rollers, cause considerable damage by chewing stems and foliage. Synthetics, such as Diazinon and Carbaryl (Sevin), will take care of most of these pests. For sucking insects, like aphid, scale, mealybug, and red spiders, that pierce the foliage and take juices from the stems and leaves, use pyrethrum; if this doesn't work, Malathion is an alternate control.

Snails and slugs are ugly pests that chew holes in leaves, but they are easily controlled. Use one of the snail-baits that contains metaldehyde, but do not apply any metaldehyde products that contain arsenicals.

With all pesticides check labels carefully to see what the product really contains and avoid the persistent hydrocarbons, as mentioned earlier.

132

Fungus diseases are unsightly infections, such as black spots on leaves and crow rot on leaves that turn gray and watery. Dust plants with sulfur and reduce moisture considerably. Botrytis blight causes gray mold on foliage and flowers; it is best to discard the infected plants. Also discard plants that develop spots, circles, or streaks of black, silver, or green on leaves or stalks. These marks may be caused by virus, and it is better to destroy plants than to cope with the unknown.

With diseased plants send adequate specimens of the plant with a written explanation to your state agricultural experimental station for diagnosis and treatment. (See end of book for listings.)

PRUNING

Learn to prune properly because it is important for successful gardening. It helps shape plants, promotes growth, and contributes to the general good looks of the landscape. Storm-broken branches

Pyrethrum is a natural insecticide; it is made from these daisylike flowers, dried and powdered. Photo courtesy of United States Department of Agriculture.

Pruning shears are a necessary garden tool for many uses; note the safety latch on these. Photo courtesy of Seymour Smith & Sons.

and overgrown shrubs are easily seen in winter when foliage is gone. Prune out dead branches or infected and diseased limbs immediately to preserve and protect the health of the plant.

Use clean, sharp tools to cut cleanly. Apply wound paint to heavy trees and shrubs after pruning. The amount of cutting varies with different plants and their stage of development. Young shade trees must be pruned so that they will have strong frameworks. Cut out crossed branches, and in general strive to keep the tree an attractive shape. Cut branches flush with the trunk; there should be no stubs. Do not prune when wood is frozen or brittle.

Large shade trees with heavy branches should be handled by a professional; it is to risky to climb ladders and wrestle with heavy limbs.

Shrubs that flower on wood from previous years can be pruned immediately after they bloom in the spring or summer. Cut away

134

weak shoots and awkward branches. Let light and air circulate so that the tree or shrub will have strong growth and flowering branches for the following seasons. Shrubs that flower on current wood need pruning in the winter or very early spring. Cut them back drastically.

Use discretion when pruning shrubs grown for ornamental fruit. Remove only dead branches, and otherwise just thin out the plant in early spring. It is best not to prune evergreen shrubs like boxwood.

Fruit trees need pruning in very late winter or in early spring. Young trees need only light cutting. Mature trees should be kept moderate in height, so that they are easy to spray and harvest.

Species roses need thinning after flowering in the summer; cut away weak and old branches. Cut climbers and ramblers at the same time, but leave as many strong new canes as possible. Prune hybrid teas in the spring; cut away dead, weak wood and crowded stems.

A good sturdy pruning saw such as this is ideal for cutting small branches and trimming trees. Photo courtesy of Seymour Smith & Sons.

Follow these rules for pruning:

1. After making a cut, apply wound paint (available at hardware stores).
2. Do not leave stubs; infection can enter.
3. Prune from the ground whenever possible.
4. On small trees cut away crossed branches.
5. Do not let a main trunk divide into a fork; remove one branch.
6. Cut away dead limbs, for they are an invitation to rot and disease.
7. Don't cut a heavy limb with one cut because it will pull the bark from the tree. Make three cuts at different places.
8. Prune just slightly above a bud.
9. Always wear gloves, and use sharp, clean tools.

TOOLS AND EQUIPMENT

Special tools and equipment and power mowers are not necessary for the average site. Don't stock a cabinet of insecticides or fertilizers; wait until you need them, and then buy them from your local nurseryman. He knows what is going on in gardening in your area and will recommend the appropriate chemicals.

Basic tools—trowel, spading fork, spade, rake, hoe—are necessities. For watering you need one or two good garden hoses, an oscillating sprinkler, a nozzle, and a watering can. For removing weeds and general cutting, keep on hand a good, sharp butcher knife, plant scissors, heavy-duty pruner, mower, and hedge clippers (power or hand). For moving soil and large plants, have a wheelbarrow or some sort of garden cart.

WHERE TO BUY PLANTS

A great many annuals and perennials are at local nurseries at planting season. In addition, mail order suppliers offer hundreds of varieties for your selection. Shrubs and trees can be ordered from your nursery or from mail order suppliers throughout the country. However, many of the smaller bulbs are difficult to find even at large garden centers, and will have to be purchased from mail order companies.

The list of mail order suppliers that follows is by no means complete (see garden magazines for others). It is merely the ones I have personally dealt with through the years and found to be very satisfactory.

Burgess Seed & Plant Co. *Annuals, perennials, seeds.*
67 E. Battle Creek Street,
Galesburg, Mich. 49053

W. Atlee Burpee Co. *All kinds of plants.*
Philadelphia, Pa. 19132
Riverside, Calif. 92502

P. De Jager & Sons, Inc. *Outstanding selection of*
188 Asbury Street, *bulbs.*
S. Hamilton, Mass. 10982

Henry Field Seed & Nursery Co. *Many kinds of landscape*
Shenandoah, Iowa 51601 *plants.*

Inter State Nurseries *Good selection of landscape*
Hamburg, Iowa 51640 *plants.*

Geo. W. Park Seed Co. *Large selection of annuals,*
Greenwood, South Carolina 29646 *perennials.*

Wayside Gardens *All kinds of landscaping*
Mentor, Ohio 44060 *plants.*

HELPFUL READING

Art of Home Landscaping, Garret Eckbo, McGraw-Hill, 1956.

Complete Illustrated Book of Garden Magic, Edited by
Marjorie Dietz, Doubleday/Ferguson, 1969.

Gardening From the Ground Up, Stanley Schiler, Macmillan, 1968.

On Gardens and Gardening, Lanning Roper, Harper & Row, 1970.

Patio Gardening, Jack Kramer, G. P. Putnam's Sons, 1970.

Planning & Planting Your Own Property, Alice Recknagel Ireys,
Wm. Morrow & Co., 1968.

Room Outside, John Brookes, Viking, 1970.

Shrubs & Vines for American Gardens, Donald Wyman, Macmillan,
Rev. Edition, 1968.

Small City Gardens, Wm. S. Brett and Kay Grant,
Abelard-Schuman, 1967.

Trees for Architecture and Landscape, Robert L. Zion,
Reinhold, 1968.

Trees for American Gardens, Donald Wyman, Macmillan, 1968.

LANDSCAPE SUPPLIES

A host of patio pavings and supplies is at local garden centers and at nurseries. Building material suppliers also carry various kinds of pavings. Consult the yellow pages of your phone book for nearest dealers.

Materials for overheads and enclosures are generally at lumberyards or general material supply places.

STATE AGRICULTURAL EXTENSION SERVICES

This service is a combined effort of the county government, the state college or university responsible for agriculture, and the United States Department of Agriculture. Telephone and addresses for these services will be found under the county government listing in your local phone books. The Agricultural Extension Service is the most up-to-date and extensive source of information on horticultural subjects in the United States. Circulars or bulletins answering frequently asked gardening questions are generally available in printed form for the asking. Addresses of these offices follow:

Agricultural Information
Auburn University
Auburn, Alabama 36830

University of Alaska
College, Alaska 99701

College of Agriculture
University of Arizona
Tucson, Arizona 85721

University of Arkansas
Box 391
Little Rock, Arkansas 72203

Agricultural Extension Service
2200 University Ave.
Berkeley, California 94720

Colorado State University
Fort Collins, Colorado 80521

College of Agriculture
University of Connecticut
Storrs, Connecticut 06268

College of Agricultural
  Sciences
University of Delaware
Newark, Delaware 19711

University of Florida
217 Rolfs Hall
Gainesville, Florida 32601

College of Agriculture
University of Georgia
Athens, Georgia 30602

University of Hawaii
2500 Dole St.
Honolulu, Hawaii 96822

College of Agriculture
University of Idaho
Moscow, Idaho 83843

College of Agriculture
University of Illinois
Urbana, Illinois 61801

Agricultural Administration
  Building
Purdue University
Lafayette, Indiana 47907

Iowa State University
Ames, Iowa 50010

Kansas State University
Manhattan, Kansas 66502

College of Agriculture
University of Kentucky
Lexington, Kentucky 40506

Louisiana State University
Knapp Hall, University Station
Baton Rouge, Louisiana 70803

Department of Public Info.
University of Maine
Orono, Maine 04473

University of Maryland
Agricultural Division
College Park, Maryland 20742

Stockbridge Hall
University of Massachusetts
Amherst, Massachusetts 01002

Dept. of Information Service
109 Agricultural Hall
East Lansing, Michigan 48823

Institute of Agriculture
University of Minnesota
St. Paul, Minnesota 55101

Mississippi State University
State College, Mississippi 39762

1-98 Agricultural Building
University of Missouri
Columbia, Missouri 65201

Office of Information
Montana State University
Bozeman, Montana 59715

Dept. of Information
College of Agriculture
University of Nebraska
Lincoln, Nebraska 68503

Agricultural Communications
   Service
University of Nevada
Reno, Nevada 89507

Schofield Hall
University of New Hampshire
Durham, New Hampshire 03824

College of Agriculture
Rutgers, State University
New Brunswick, New Jersey 08903

New Mexico State University
Drawer 3A1
Las Cruces, New Mexico 88001

State College of Agriculture
Cornell University
Ithaca, New York 14850

North Carolina State University
State College Station
Raleigh, North Carolina 27607

North Dakota State University
State University Station
Fargo, North Dakota 58102

Cooperative Extension Service
Ohio State University
2120 Fyffe Road
Columbus, Ohio 43210

Oklahoma State University
Stillwater, Oklahoma 74074

Oregon State University
206 Waldo Hall
Corvallis, Oregon 97331

Pennsylvania State University
Armsby Bldg. Room 1
University Park, Pennsylvania 16802

University of Rhode Island
16 Woodwall Hall
Kingston, Rhode Island 02881

Clemson University
Clemson, South Carolina 29631

South Dakota State University
University Station
Brookings, South Dakota 57006

University of Tennesseee
Box 1071
Knoxville, Tennessee 37901

Texas A & M University
Services Building
College Station, Texas 77843

Utah State University
Logan, Utah 84321

University of Vermont
Burlington, Vermont 05401

Virginia Polytechnic Inst.
Blacksburg, Virginia 24061

Washington State University
115 Wilson Hall
Pullman, Washington 99163

West Virginia University
Evansdale Campus
Appalachian Center
Morgantown, West Virginia   26506

University of Wisconsin
Madison, Wisconsin   53706

University of Wyoming
Box 3354
Laramie, Wyoming   82070

Federal Extension Service
U. S. Dept. of Agriculture
Washington, D.C.   20250